C000258948

NOISE

NOISE

A MANIFESTO MODERNISING
MOTHERHOOD

DANUSIA MALINA-DERBEN

First published in 2021 by
TRIUMPH PRESS
Kemp House
152–160 City Road
London EC1V 2NXY
www.triumphpress.co

Typeset in Garamond by MacGuru Ltd
Printed and bound in Great Britain by CPI Group (UK) Ltd

The moral right of the author has been asserted.

ISBN 978 1 83820 980 3

For mothers; whichever version of motherhood belongs to you.

Contents

Introduction

To tell you this is a book about motherhood is both a statement and a little bit of a lie because it's not the type of book about motherhood you'll be used to picking up from the self-development shelves. I know this because I've been the woman picking up those books for decades now.

While everything I've set out to achieve in writing this book is wrapped up in being a mother, it's also about how we're *not* allowed to be mothers. Or more accurately, how once we become mothers, we're not allowed to be *ourselves*. I've searched high and low in the literature about being a mother that takes this tricky question – *how do I be a mother and still be me?* – and fruitfully answers it. Or at least, opens a more comprehensive conversation on what it takes to be a mother and yourself across our modern societies that go beyond Sunday morning yoga and scented candles.

In the following chapters, that's what I've

aimed to do. This isn't a self-help book, and it doesn't have all the answers. I'm not going to be telling you how to do *this* or achieve *that* or find yourself amongst the chaos. It's a manifesto, *my* manifesto, to start a conversation. To get the ideas flowing through our communities and to see what discussions can be opened from those ideas. It's an encouragement to think differently from what we're repeatedly told about motherhood so we can make a change for ourselves and our children.

Motherhood is wrapped in various cultural meanings, and it's led to a conflation of what it means to be 'feminine' and 'maternal'. The Collins Dictionary defines this word motherhood as *"the state of being a mother"*. A state then, described as *"the particular condition that someone or something is in at a specific time"*. Additionally, and crucially, the term "mother" is a gendered term and is consequently limited by gender, and I want to acknowledge that trans, non-binary, and gender-queer birthing people are not represented either by the title of this book or consistently by its content.

Our differences matter, and we are not all the same. I acknowledge the social, historical, economic and political contexts of our differences and how they impact how we both choose and are allowed to determine what the 'state' of being a mother will look like for us. Our varying cultures and circumstances mean all families live and love differently. Which is why I'll fill in the census boxes with what those circumstances look like for me – not to excuse or make justification through acknowledging them – but so you know the platform(s) from which I'm speaking. That way, you can make your own decisions about which ideas to move forward with and which ones aren't for you. As I said, I'm not here to tell you what to do or give you any formulaic answers, because that's crass. I'm here to connect and have a conversation – a new one, about motherhood.

My position is situated in the Western world, both socio-culturally and historically, and I occupy multiple social categories: gender (cisgender), ethnicity (White British), race (White), sexuality (primarily cis-het) age (midlife), nationality (British) and class (established middle). These shape my experiences and the expectations I speak of here.

To build that platform even more, and share with you the nuances of my life as a mother, there's also my reality of being a single mother of a large family (adult, teen and young children) which includes those who are disabled and higher-order multiples, triplets. Whilst there's no physical co-parenting, financial support is present. Since becoming a single parent, this included (at different times) state benefits such as child benefit, disabled living allowance, housing benefit and tax credits. I share this because it's all too easy to hide intertwined circumstances. Being successful in running a business, with a team to support, lives side by side with financial vulnerability. For instance, renting a home rather than owning one is for many single mothers (including me) a reality. If we back-glance, I was originally adopted from an orphanage, into an entrepreneurial immigrant/British established-middle-class family, and I'm highly educated. I've since connected with my birth family, and their experiences, while not ones I had growing up, also inform and shape the ways I feel about myself and motherhood. Of course, it can be compelling to lean on binary thinking (successful <u>or</u> unsuccessful, strong <u>or</u> weak, winner <u>or</u> victim), but what I'm sharing here is far more intricate and multidimensional.

Taking all our cultural experiences into account, I believe our unwavering desire to create meaningful, prosperous lives for ourselves and our children is the same. There is a commonality that exists for us, that accounts for all the myriads of platforms we find ourselves balancing on, that says we want to be mothers, but we also want to be *us*. I'm tired of this version of motherhood that keeps telling us we can't have both or that we can 'have-it-all' (not at the same time) but only within the safe constructs of the narratives that already exist around motherhood. I've been listening to it for too long, and I know there is a better way forward.

Dictionary definitions aside, motherhood

should not be a 'state'; it's something we each come to, learn from, adapt to and from, and build into our lives in idiosyncratic ways. Our personal histories and the histories of the communities around us all inform how we think and feel about being a mother. It's NOISE – something we're going to talk about a lot throughout this book.

I've written this manifesto because modernising how we think, speak, and feel about motherhood is long overdue. I've said it's *my* manifesto and I'm hoping once you finish, it'll inform what you choose as *your* manifesto too.

It's my seventeenth birthday, and I'm sitting on a loo, holding a double-lined pregnancy test in my hand.

This is how my journey into motherhood began. Shock doesn't cover it.

My mother drags me to a consultant for an immediate termination. She throws down evidence of my burgeoning dance and drama successes and the impossibility of an ongoing pregnancy. Her voice pierces the room, even as she's met with the level consideration that my wishes need to be included. This is new to her because, after all, she knows what I need more than I do. The consultant, patience thinned, checks his paperwork for my age. Once he's confident I'm old enough to have a say, he orders my mother from the room. It takes four insistences of "OUT!" before she clutches her bag to her chest and marches to close the door behind her. Flounce was made for that moment.

"Now, Danusia. What do YOU want to do

about this pregnancy?" he asks, once we're alone. As soon as I say I have no intention of not having the baby, he calls my mother back to share what the path forward will be for me; ante-natal care and delivery would, like it or not, go ahead.

Both my parents were resolute; I was made for 'better things'. Becoming a single, teenage mother would be the ruin of me. The shame I brought to the family was deepened by their feelings about the sheer waste of all the years of developing me as a Royal Ballet regional scholar and Italia Conti drama school scholar. I was supposed to be more than a no hope-teenage mother. This rocked their already fractious marriage.

My mother pursed her lips, shook her lowered head side to side and picked up knitting patterns, her needles and pastel yellow wool. My illegitimate child was destined to have the best homemade layette, ever. My father decided to be mute from the day I broke the baby news, through the pregnancy, and into the blue light dash to the hospital. Even once I returned home with a healthy baby boy in my arms, his habit of looking through me became an art. In this stonewalling stretch, he *didn't say one single word directly to me. I was damaged goods. His disappointment festered foul in the fabric of my childhood home.*

One thing was made clear. Everything to do with my baby had to be done by me. They both refused to help in all ways. A child looking after another. Seventeen and breastfeeding, lapsed A levels and a seemingly broken future.

Why I Had to Write This Book

I never wanted to write this book. It's not something I hoped I'd have to do. I've spent more years than I can remember checking out bookstores flicking through, and buying books on motherhood *because*, fingers crossed, someone else would write it.

Because of my steady book-buying on all things' motherhood, my shelves are laden with everything from raw memoirs to how-to guides and onto academic texts around this question of motherhood. Writings on motherhood have moved beyond sanitised versions where everything is beautiful, pretty and, the all-important, picture of togetherness (Instagram excepted). Thankfully, there are now brilliant, expansive writings on the inside track of the hell, the joy, the mess, the treachery, the grief, the ecstasy, the darkness, and the isolation, the desolation and the heart-swelling gloriousness of being a mother. Like so many of us, I've looked for answers to the bottomless-pit-of-questions that motherhood brings. I'm talking about practical solutions to parenting, understanding and raising happy kids, and the ever-present challenges of juggling, life-balance and fulfilment as a working woman, who also has children.

I'm now a working mother of ten, a long way from that scared teen mum, who delivered her firstborn alone. From that day as a seventeen-year-old to my last children's birth (triplets in my late forties), I've been trying to answer, amongst the daily chaos and minutiae of domestic life, the same grinding never-ending fucking questions. And while I've been asked to speak on stages about my success at garnering career accomplishments with my brood of children, it's become evident that this rests on *basic assumptions about what it takes to be a mother.* The fact that I am dressed in day clothes rather than nightwear speaks to a version of motherhood that is pervasive.

So, I set out to reconsider my career as a working mother and exactly what questions throughout these decades have dogged and continue to dog the experience. For five years, I was a pregnant/breastfeeding stay at home mother, before I entered paid work and studied within higher education. Degrees later, I became an academic and from there, an entrepreneur, a consultant in the corporate world, and podcast host. For more than three decades, I've juggled work with young children. None of this is to position myself as Super Woman. This moniker and stereotype aren't accurate, and neither is it helpful because if nothing else it obscures the complexities of what it's taken to raise children as a working mother. It's blatant theatrics to collude in this Super Woman picture. Paradoxically, it's not been a single-handed endeavour. Still, in many ways, it's the crippling, solitary responsibility of motherhood that made me both not want to share my observations **and** know that I must do precisely that.

In an act of cowardice (and forgivable at-capacity bandwidth) I previously hoped someone else would unpack the central propositions of modern motherhood in the ways I need them to be undone – critiqued if you like. It wasn't until I experienced the extremity of triplet motherhood that the penny dropped. *"If there's a book that you want to read, but it hasn't been written yet, then you must write it"*, as iconic feminist writer Toni Morrison puts it.

Over the past few years, the ambivalence of motherhood has been repeatedly described in a way that forces us to take motherhood writing (and motherhood itself), as Lauren Elkin describes, *"from a niche concern to the serious, pressing, and universal subject that it is"*. I want to re-examine core pillars of motherhood that *appear* taken for granted, despite the wealth of debate about them; the propositions mothers write and speak about as if they are gospel. It's my wish here to point to the gospel that might not need to be this way and to present ways to unfix them.

If I were to boil this down to a core concern that dominated and still dominates my mothering and what I see driven into motherhood, is this one question: **HOW CAN I BE ME AND BE A MOTHER?** Or if you want a slightly more highfalutin version: **How can I be a success (in my own right) and be a mother?** This inquiry has been active from the nanosecond I found out I was pregnant to this day and it strikes at the heart of what is still to be said about motherhood. I believe this work is urgent if we are not to replicate the distressed world we live in. Mothers have a profound power to shape change and shake things up for a better, freer society.

But first; what this book is and isn't

This book isn't a memoir of my motherhood life, even though I share fragmentary moments with you. It's not a formula on how to be a good or better mother – there are more than enough books telling us how we ought to be, and what we ought to do (more on this to follow). It's not a 'fixing' of women either.

It is a conversation-starting exploration from what I call informal research and which Eve Rodsky, during a School for Mothers podcast conversation with me, describes well when she says *"all research is me-search"*.

In my academic career, I spent years conducting research and then carving out leadership theories. Sometimes I've viewed this book as the findings of an exploratory long-term research project into "modern motherhood" with patterns stretched over decades, as I've gone in and out of different stages of motherhood. As one stage ended for one child, it began for another – over and over and over again. I've seen trends and fads galore, but the core question about what it takes to be yourself, raise children and do fulfilling work never disappears. I'm not talking about life balance here; it goes well beyond this. Instead, it's about that torturous problem of how to maintain (and ideally grow) my sense of self while raising {loads of} kids, <u>and</u> at the same time pursue work that is, remotely, matched to my talents/ambitions. Pass the bucket. Hand me an axe to chuck. It's my response to this unerring 'life project' that's the stuff of my research.

This isn't a pure research project, albeit there are autoethnographical elements to it; the following chapters are what I've learnt in my journey so far, but they're not final findings, by any means. Remember: 1. My children are not all grown and flown, and 2. It's questionable if/when the impacts of (grand) motherhood might ever quell. As one of my PhD supervisors, Professor Judi Marshall mentions, we "*as a society are not used to tolerating experiments publicly*" and "*women need safe environments in which to make their more daring trials of who they are*". This book isn't necessarily a safe environment, but it's a necessary one.

There's a quick aside to take care of before we move on. During writing this book, I was asked, by a PR company owner, whether I'd be including other women's words, experiences and/or testimony here. Not an unusual query. Scratching below the surface of this basic question, I discovered she was fixed on the notion that unless others back my thoughts, these run the danger of being 'mere hearsay'. Quite the proposition despite Muriel Rukeyser's words that "*what would happen if one woman told the truth about her life? The world would split open*". I couldn't help be reminded of critiques of feminist researchers who in the past were deemed not to meet 'traditional standards' aka masculinist approaches of validity and were therefore accused of being engaged in "sloppy research". Margaret Gearty and Judi Marshall talk about this as they discuss how *"charges of ruminative self-indulgence can spar with ripostes of worthwhile, investigative self-expression"* – an instructive tension, for sure.

There are dangers to: 1. Putting forward what some might call 'navel-gazing' observations, and 2. Converting these into generalisable claims. Nonetheless, my life observations' and their 'trustworthiness' are not to be discarded. I'm not applying my findings to construct universal theories, and I certainly don't assume insulting and damaging applicability. The thing is, I can't predict nor want to predict how my observations and thoughts on the central tenets of my motherhood will land with you. If these provoke thought and encourage us all to reconsider, discuss and confirm beliefs about motherhood, there's the chance for change if and where it's needed.

So far, I've talked about how my motherhood journey forms the underlying spur to this book; I'm yet to share the specificity of this with you which is important because as Alexis Pauline

Gumbs puts forward, "*we are accountable when we are specific*".

I want to be clear that the underpinnings of motherhood that I'm questioning and bringing to your attention, are not necessarily experienced in the same way by everyone. The themes may be well-known ones, but that doesn't mean the ways they play out for each mother are identical or even present. Motherhood is <u>not</u> a universal experience. The experiences I have as a mother, with the systems of power that affect me positively and negatively, aren't the same as a mother who faces different power systems.

Many feminisms assume motherhood is this unitary (ontological) position or identity that affects all the people placed as women in the same ways. Thinking about motherhood in this way limits the impact factors, like race, disability, neuro-normativity, class, and sexuality have on mothers. It centres a version of motherhood that is more often than not, white. Being blunt, mothering has been coded as white mothering. The majority of 'good mothering' literature is told by white, middle-class mothers, like me.

Except motherhood occurs within the intersecting structures of race, ethnicity, social class, ableism, and sexuality. Zoe Darwin and Mari Greenfield note that "*we have not yet developed shared language in research or practice to adequately describe reproductive histories outside of a cis birth mother's*". Unfortunately, much of the literature on mothers and mothering assumes white, middle-class values and experiences. It's no longer acceptable to reel off a list of privileges in an attempt to acknowledge said privilege. The narrative of the "superiority" of whiteness is pervasive to the point where it shapes the master narrative and the way we read the world, including motherhood. There are arguments that feminism constitutes some vague understanding of 'empowerment', and that this idea of empowerment is actually immune from questions like, whose empowerment are we talking about and to what end? Is feminism a luxury for those who can afford it? Does feminism as it stands genuinely integrate the needs and concerns of mothers as people? Of mothers of colour? Working-class mothers?

Disabled mothers? Neuro-diverse mothers? Queer mothers? Trans mothers?

Modernising motherhood has everything to do with intersectionality because no mother is free until all mothers are free. But frankly, who wants **any** mothers to be free and liberated? As it stands, our perfect 'ideal' motherhood is so wrapped up in white, able-bodied, middle class, cisgender, hetero-normative, neuro-normative motherhood, it can't possibly represent all women. Instead, we operate in factions; our differences creating neatly drawn lines between us. Kimberle Crenshaw in naming intersectionality broke the news to women like me that, *"when they enter, we all enter"*. Whereas men can (apparently) be the template of human, white women must not be, and are not, the template of perfect motherhood.

My aim is to move the conversation forward on motherhood themes while not deepening normative notions about motherhood that don't serve us. They don't serve women. They don't serve mothers. They damage mothers of colour and marginalised mothers. In the eyes of patriarchy, not all mothers are created equal, to the point where some women are not thought of as mothers and are therefore not extended the courtesy of having their mothering scrutinised through this patriarchal institution in the first place. Plus, many do the labour of mothering without the luxury of motherhood status; it's a category of citizenship many are denied. Alongside this, the LGBTQAI community face barriers to parenting and legal hoops that restrict them access to the people they mother, taken for granted by others.

Deep-seated racism means that mothers of colour are failed repeatedly. For example, Black women are five times more likely to die in childbirth than white women, and Asian women are twice as likely (MBRRACE, 2019). Black mothers are slandered as they are positioned heinously as the liability harming the life chances of Black people (Black in America, CNN) as internalised racism reinforces the existence of a larger story that tells of the unmoving nature of ideological whiteness. Additionally, Black mothers navigate, as Marie Dow puts it "*two controlling images of motherhood… the Welfare Queen and the SBW (Strong Black Woman)"* – negative perceptions concerning so-called "styles of motherhood" that deviate from the norm. The experience of mothering through the prism of Blackness in a racialised context is entirely different from mothering as a white middle-class woman.

Concepts of motherhood are damaging for a host of groups of women. I'd go so far as to say they are damaging for *all* women. Motherhood is <u>not</u> a monolithic experience, as I've said, the diversity of motherhood must be acknowledged. My observations cannot hope to lift the lid on these multiplicities, but can speak to the ways I've found enduring (whitewashed) versions of motherhood to be unsatisfactory as a white woman, and how I've attempted to resist these versions. In *Practicing Feminist Mothering* (2012), Fiona Joy Green describes feminist pedagogy as challenging what is seen to be obvious, the natural, the accepted, and the unquestioned. I cannot speak for others, but I can speak to my lived experience, trouble it and make sense of it, where possible. I'm sick of motherhood writing, especially of the how-to variety, teaching mothers to be happier in the prison, rather than calling out the prison itself.

This book is shortish because, need I repeat: *working mother of ten, including triplets (!)*. I'm kind of joking except that being time-poor is one of the hallmarks of working mothers. To surmount the psychological distress of completing a book while running a business, hosting two podcasts, raising young kids (including disabled ones), I started calling this book a pamphlet which alleviated some pressure. I also soothed myself with the idea that readers might not have time to plough through a massive tome on motherhood. I am/was too busy busting my arse, making it all hold together to get concerned about measuring up to a standardised book-length. I needed to do what I could for me, while getting messages pressing on my heart out. But so often, women with young children can't find space (time *and* head) to immerse in book writing. That word **immerse** makes me howl because unless mother-writers are mega

resourced, with money and support for starters, then when exactly can we ever immerse?
It's long been acknowledged that the conditions under which mother-writers produce are
a far cry from male writers. Note: I didn't say
father writers with help-mate wives. To pri-
oritise creative expression over the traditional
~~duties~~ role of spouse, mother and homemaker
requires constant choices about others' needs
and our own ambitions. Layered on the subject
of motherhood is the need to transcend it to
write about it – quite the irony, and one that
mother-writers grapple with.

I've found myself hungry for stories of how
others pull it off – writing and motherhood.
Do they write in the dead of night, children
and partner snoring in bed? Do they write every
day, a set amount chipping away so that the
book is, *voila*, written one day? Do they escape
to a hotel room, a cabin, rent a spare room for a
fortnight and write furiously in bedclothes with
stinky hair and nothing but biscuits to live on?
Do they down alcohol copiously to capture
the muse and/or to avoid the internal pain

of anticipated hatred of their work? It's documented that Maya Angelou wrote in a "tiny mean" hotel room, surrounded by a dictionary, a Bible, a deck of cards, and a bottle of sherry. Me? A mish-mash of trials of production from late-night writing followed by ambrosial hour (4–6 am) sessions. I wrote surrounded by children at home, or in bed, never anything but black Earl Grey tea to help me through. I could not afford the luxury of a regular schedule even though I had to hold to a fanatical commitment to produce this work or it would not get done. I kept telling myself, the conditions for creativity will never ever be ideal, right?! I've never subscribed to the fiction within works of fiction that Grace Eliot remarks on *"to create a life is to abandon the creative pursuits I've always seen as my life's work"*. Stories of women who must give up their creativity to be mothers, or who lose their ability to create in the fog of having children are all part of why I had to write this book.

This is a manifesto. **Manifesto** (noun): a written statement declaring publicly the intentions, motives, or views of its issuer – that would be me on motherhood!

It's a manifesto because I'm not writing this to teach mothers how to thrive within the understandings of motherhood that already exist. It's about the way that I've come to understand what's being asked of me and how I've needed to adjust crucial central pillars within motherhood so that I can thrive. I've needed to act in my favour to make motherhood better. It's this self-advocacy for a better version of motherhood that may, or may not, hold clues for you too.

A Short Note on Using this Book
The following chapters are laid out into three sections:

1. Hearing the NOISE: A short piece of memoir (a micro-memoir, of a sort), where I share some of my own experiences of motherhood with you.
2. Exploring the NOISE: Thoughts and context around six core pillars of

motherhood we're held accountable to, that I've identified. This is where I dive deeper into and unpack the writings, research and lived experiences, that currently inform the ways we think about motherhood.

3. Questioning the NOISE: This is where I hand it back to you. At the end of each chapter, you'll find a short summary and exploratory questions for you to take the conversation further.

As I've said, I'm not here to tell you how to do this or give you a magic formula. This is to let you know what to expect. How you approach it from here, is entirely up to you.

You could, for instance, choose to read the memoir bits for now and the rest later. You could skip the memoir altogether and get stuck straight into the context bits. Then again, you could explore the questions as you go or read the book, sit with it a while, and then come back to the questions when you're ready. Read it alone in one sitting, or spread it out over however long it takes you to find the space to read it – whether that's a week or a year. You could read it with friends or family or as part of a book club.

All this to say, do whatever suits you with this book. Throw it out the window if that's what you feel called to do! Of course, I'd prefer it if you didn't do that and that you'll find a way to let this book do what I hope it will – start a conversation. With yourself and with others.

Married at eighteen and the mother of four sons by twenty-two. During my fourth pregnancy, I was growing a new human, stripping back multi-layered legacies of paint on the banisters of the cheapest, biggest, coldest house my husband and I could afford, while doing everything I thought best to be the kind of mummy my kids needed.

My life consisted of cooking fresh meals, knitting kids jumpers, playing puzzles and games with wooden toys, weeding the garden, reading bedtime books, and organising playdates for each child. Alongside community volunteering for me, sex with my husband every other day, and keeping groomed as much as I could manage in between the busy lives of the people I'd created and loved. Everything I needed was close by: my kids, my hubby, and the dankest heaviest of feelings that there was something more.

Starting a mother's group in my home was meant to cast off the blistering loneliness lodged in every day that ended with 'y'. And it did, in the beginning. Working in the Women's Aid shelter opened my eyes to a world I didn't know existed for so many women. And my love grew for people my mother whisperingly called 'the fallen', a category never far from my recently legitimised status since marriage. Starting in the Probation Service, working directly with offenders brought disadvantage to my door. As much as I asked them to stop bringing me 'gifts' which I thought sweet at first, I wised up that I was inadvertently accepting stolen goods. At least this was relief from the blindingly repetitive time sink of motherhood.

I was told, 'this is IT now' on replay everywhere I went. This is it now for you was also "there'll be time for you when they're gone" as well as "you were made to be a mother" which often morphed into "you must be proud of them all, biggest achievement right there in front of you". Being proud of my sons was not enough to rest my life up against. I was crying secretly for confirmation that my life was anything but done. These little sparks I cherished were apparently ripe for the future. I was not only the architect of this build out for them, I was expected to wait in the wings, cheering them on while I gained absolute satisfaction from serving up their futures.

This was the IT of my life. The reason to wake each day involved making the beds, washing chubby faces, getting laundry done and ironed, making and feeding them meals, shopping for food and the house, scratching over bills, robbing one credit card to pay the other, having sex once the kids were e.v.e.n.t.u.a.l.l.y asleep, stripping head lice, pushing swings and steely roundabouts in the cold, visiting family, always smiling. Knowing all along that this was IT. This is what I was told my life was meant to be about. I listened. I heard the same message. I listened for new messages, just in case, by some fluke, I'd misunderstood. But the story kept coming back the same.

You're a mother. Know your place.

Unravelling the NOISE and
MOTHER STOPPER Culture

As Aurelie Athan tells us, *"the mother is the beginning of everything yet she's often the last called to the table"*. All through my life as a mother, I've encountered what I began to call Noise; the unending cacophony about what it means to be a mother, how I should behave and what's possible for me because I have children. I've been subject to this maternal focused Noise for longer than many women because of the extended and extreme timeframe of my raising children.

I'm deeply familiar with the Noise of a certain kind of motherhood, framed from within the structures of power I occupy. I imagine you are too, although yours and mine won't necessarily replicate one another.

Noise (noun): *"refers to the unwanted parts of a situation, especially ones that make it more difficult for you to do or understand something"* (Collins Dictionary). Noise is the cacophony that drowns women out. It surrounds women with what must happen, what you can do, what you can't do, what you can be, what you can't be. It's there when you're not a mother, but it grows into an off-key orchestral racket when you are.

The pressure on mothers is Noise. Loud, low, quiet, a blur, fuzzy, insistent. Or as David Perell suggests, *"a self-reinforcing cycle that creates collective beliefs. An idea will gain traction once it enters the mainstream, which triggers a chain reaction, which causes lots of people to adopt it not because it's true but because it's popular"*. The Noise becomes beliefs, which become rules, so they become dominant narratives and conventional wisdom as if they are 'true'. It's the racket that we put up with once we become mothers. As if in producing the future generation we become 'public property' in relation to a societal monitoring vigilance that tells us how to behave, how to dress, what to be concerned about, what is best for us and best for our children, how to live, and to accept opinions and advice from others as if truth.

I needed to identify the Noise that affected me because I could feel it was somehow unavoidable where motherhood was concerned. The Noise told me I needed and should be a certain kind of person now that I'm a mother. I thought I had to believe what the Noise told me to believe. Before I knew it, I was hearing this Noise day in, day out, both externally <u>and</u> internally, because I'd ingested it, replayed it back to myself and regurgitated it out to others. It was almost impossible to hang onto any sense of self. I was at risk of turning into what the Noise told me and therefore, I began to lose who I was and what I wanted. I couldn't think beyond my Noise. Everything begins with a narrative and the more we understand which narratives are driving what, the more human we'll all be.

This book is borne *"out of an insistence to counter whatever narrative is given to me as the truth when it doesn't resonate or sit right"*, as Emily Rapp Black neatly tells us. It is borne out of a version of motherhood that doesn't sit right with me. A version that annihilates many women. A version that stops us in our tracks. The Noise is a symptom of a culture that simply doesn't want mothers to succeed in our own right. I've come to call this the **Mother Stopper Culture**.

We live in this Mother Stopper culture. We can (before we get pregnant) *feel* as if we have equal opportunity. Though not probable, it's possible that childless women who aren't of low income, disabled, queer, or women of colour see the world as their oyster. The point at which we become pregnant is when we hit Mother Stoppers.

Chunky in-the-way Mother Stoppers.

Mother Stoppers are those people with 'helpful' advice and opinions about us once we're pregnant. Advice about food, drinks and activities we can no longer take part in, because, *the baby*. Mother Stoppers are workplace managers jumping to conclusions about our commitment to the company, our work and our career. They're medical interventions that place us on a rollercoaster of (mostly but not always helpful) care. They're experts on maternity, baby kits, baby sleeping, child psy-cho-social-emotional development, birthing, paternity advice, and that's just the beginning. Everyone, including strangers, seems to take up their 'right' to comment on what becomes a public event, even when this is a private one.

This isn't exclusive to pregnancy and the baby stage. Mother Stoppers keep on coming; the maternal wall, gender pay gap, lack of affordable childcare or availability of childcare, unenforceable maintenance payments, educa-tional hours operating on assumptions of one parent available for caregiving, opt-in opt-out fathers, and more.

The Noise conditions us to think we're the ones who should do the caring, people identify-ing as women, that is. That we're the only ones who can do things 'just so'. Mother Stoppers and their Noise stops mothers from focusing on ourselves and tells us it's selfish to even want to do so, let alone actually do it. Other Noise convinces us it's an either/or situation. We can have family **or** ourselves and our dreams/desires ought to dissolve away in the face of family obligations. If we *do* feel torn between wanting a life of our own and wanting to be a mother, then we are not showing up as **good** mothers. For a white, educated middle-class woman, the Noise makes it clear we must choose a primary role: either we have careers or we raise children. One of these things must be the centre of our lives. Seriously though, the choice has been made for us. We are mothers, and everything else must stop.

Let's not blanket this, because it isn't the case for mothers of colour. Kimberley Seals Aller puts this into sharp contrast when she tells us *"there was a time when the only work options available to women of colour were doing the work that white women of means did not want to do"*. This career or children 'choice' isn't angst-filled ambivalence sitting at the core of all mother's experience. It can't be. I'll return to this later in more detail, although I'll leave a flavour of the nub here thanks again to Kimberley Seals Allers: *"let's be clear that many white women of means have achieved that balance standing on the backs of women of colour"*.

I believe there's more NOISE now than ever before.

Hard-fought progress on women's rights is under attack. In today's more divided, conservative and still male-dominated societies, there's pushback against gender equality and women's rights. This backlash is a socially pervasive phenomenon and comes in many forms including men's rights groups action against perceived advantages of women (Jordan, 2016). Pro-family and pro-life groups face a backlash against birth control and abortion (Harrison and Rowley, 2011). Much of this push back centres around reproductive rights in developed countries, including the United States and Europe. Anti-feminist groups are working to undo women's progress and re-install what they call 'the natural family unit'.

Letting the Noise in without a filter is feeding a destructive, cyclical narrative for mothers everywhere. Half the time, we don't even realise it's there because we've become so oblivious to it – or worse – we've accepted there's nothing we can do about it.

The first step in breaking this vicious cycle is to stop and **Recognise the NOISE**; how it shows up and the forms it takes. That's what this book is all about.

But first: **Let's break it down visually:**

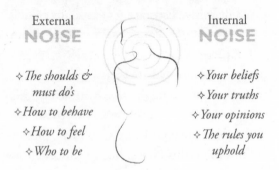

External
NOISE

⬦ *The shoulds &*
must do's
⬦ *How to behave*
⬦ *How to feel*
⬦ *Who to be*

Internal
NOISE

⬦ *Your beliefs*
⬦ *Your truths*
⬦ *Your opinions*
⬦ *The rules you*
uphold

Every mother experiences this uniquely and differently, as I've said – but we all experience it.

Whatever the composition and location of our family – even (or especially) when we have curated social media feeds of cookie-cutter lives.

Over time, the cumulative impact of all this Noise is the erosion of our sense of self. We forget who we are. We forget who we want to be. And we forget what we believe is possible for ourselves because we allow the Noise to dictate it for us.

I've put together a table (see overleaf) of some different external and internal Noise and how this might show up, though remember this isn't a definitive list since it's culturally bound.

But there's also a third column. This column is for those statements we may have said or thought about other mothers. This reflects the contributions we might also be making to the noise around us. Recognise any of these? And if not, what are your versions in each column?

I'm calling this Noise, but we already know these end up being narratives and stories that we tell ourselves or let other people tell us. Because these narratives take root in our systems, it becomes natural for us to focus on growing confirmation that they are right. That they are 'the way things must be'. We surrender to this rightness, and even if we grapple with this Noise, it's often within the confines of the framework of our beliefs.

Cue sad trombone; the ways we talk to, and

External NOISE	Internal NOISE	Adding to the NOISE
❖ When are you going back to work?	❖ My children's happiness comes before my own.	❖ I can't believe she/you hasn't cleaned her/your house before we came over.
❖ Are you really going back to work that soon?	❖ I have to do it all myself or people will think I can't cope.	❖ She/You should let her/your kids be kids and not expect them to help clean up.
❖ You can't have it all - you need to choose between your kids and your career now.	❖ I'm a bad mother. ❖ I'm a bad feminist. ❖ I can't have it all.	❖ I would never let my kids watch as much TV/ screen time the way she/you do.
❖ It's so good your partner/husband took a couple of weeks off to help out.	❖ I don't deserve to have it all. ❖ My career can come later when my children are happy.	❖ She/You needs to spend more time with the kids and less time online/at work/on herself.
❖ When are you having your second/ next baby?	❖ I should just be grateful for what I have already and stop expecting more for myself.	❖ I can't believe she/you let the kids eat McDonald's/ take-away/cake for breakfast.
❖ What a pity you couldn't breastfeed! Did you try XXX?	❖ If I focus too much on my career, what will people say?	❖ I wish my partner/ husband were as hands-on as that - she's/you're so lucky to have him.
❖ You shouldn't let your kids sleep in bed with you.		❖ I would never do things the way she/you do.
❖ You have to let your baby cry it out.		
❖ You should never let your baby cry it out.		
❖ It's all about the kids now. When they leave, you can think more about you		

about, ourselves are more powerful than we realise. Not only for the ways it makes us feel, but for the ways, we inadvertently pass this Noise onto our children which is so important if we ever want a better world.

Let's step back a moment. Our Internal Noise is a mixture of conscious and subconscious thoughts. It can (of course) be positive as well as negative, but let's face it, you know as well as I do that when it comes to being a modern mother, it's almost always negative as we're bombarded with the cacophony of that unsolicited 'advice' I talked about earlier. Isn't it interesting that so much of this unsolicited advice or feedback is constraining?!

External Noise lodges itself inside us and feeds our Internal Noise. At least that's what I had to work out, and through. And in doing this I discovered:

Negative Internal Noise falls into one of four categories:

1. *Personalising* – You blame yourself when things go wrong.

2. **Polarising** – You see things only as good or bad, no grey areas or room for middle ground.
3. **Magnifying** – You only focus on the negative in every scenario and dismiss anything good or positive.
4. **Catastrophising** – You always expect the worst possible outcome for yourself.

It may be that you identify with only one of these categories or multiple ones. The point is, once I started identifying my Noise and the narratives linked to it, my awareness inevitably began to disrupt it.

It took me a while, but I could see that some External Noise stuck to me like tar. I'd magnify it internally to the sound effect of three orchestras all playing against one another. And then, because I'm human, I'd start spouting my version of that Noise as projectile information outwards to others. Consider this as TRUTH, right there.

Want an example? Here's one that had me on my knees:

⬦ External Noise: "Good mothers give every child individual attention" (Polarising)

⬦ Internal Noise: "I'm such a shit mother because I don't give all my kids the same individual attention" (Personalising)

⬦ Contributing Noise: "Isn't it so bad when we can't give our kids individual attention?" (Magnifying)

This information is taken on by another mother who then questions whether she's doing enough because it's become a narrative, or as my friend Panagiota Skandali calls this, a *narrowtive*!

It can be tough to see outside my narrative's framework. My life as a mother is framed by Noise galore absorbed, ingested, listened to and regurgitated. To progress my/your/their rights, as opposed to the duties of mothers, I've **had** to flip these cultural scripts. This is why recognising, interrupting and cutting through the Noise has to happen. Mother Stopping Noise acts as a handbrake on the life of a powerful woman.

But disrupting existing narratives for mothers *is* possible. This work opens a world of contradictions and complexities, naturally just like any growth. It's an untangling, where there's potential to make wholly conscious decisions about the Noise we allow into our lives and *whether* we want to give a damn about it or not.

We make it OUR choice. Are you with me?

Unravelling Your NOISE

As you've hopefully picked up by now, I'm very conscious about not wanting this to be a tell-you-how-to-live-your-life kind of book. We've got enough of that Noise already (Contributing Noise: see?). I'm not going to tell you how to cut through your Noise, purely and simply, because I can't. It's *your* Noise and I've got mine. I know the solutions for me – I'm living them – but I can't give you a prescription for your own.

That might sound disheartening, but it's not. It's an opportunity. I want this to be an invitation to reflect, to go deep below the surface of all the Noise and really start to unpick the unique ways it's showing up in your life. Through this unpicking – individually and collectively – we can begin to understand our own ways through it.

What I can offer, to help you on the way, are exploratory questions. Take them or leave them. Tweak them and reframe them. Do it alone or with someone you trust. It's entirely up to you how you tackle this, but I *do* encourage you to tackle it.

Here are a few to get you started:

1. What are the most pressing Noises showing up in your life?
2. How would you categorise your Noise across External, Internal and Contributing? Which ones soothe you and which ones irritate you?
3. Which ones do you want to interrupt and cut out the most?
4. Which of the four categories for negative noise (personalising, polarising,

magnifying or catastrophising) do you tend to fall into the most when listening to the Noise?

5. Whose voices have reinforced the category you fall into most? Essentially: who are you allowing to reinforce the ways you think about yourself? Reflect on your biggest influences here: parents, wider family, friends, partner/spouse, social media/mass media.

Central Pillars of Modern Motherhood
The following chapters unpick the incessant Noise of them, all in the quest of answering: How can I be me <u>and</u> be a mother?

These are the central pillars of modern motherhood that won't be silenced. I've troubled with them for years (maybe you have too, or not one bit).

These are the Mother Stopping fuckers that just won't be quiet.

I'm a mother, and I must know my place.

I was warned that being a full-time university student and a mum of four little boys was a feat too hard to handle. This vote of unease bolstered me to reprise the saying I'd adopted when I announced I'd be getting a place at university sans A levels: "Watch me". It became my inner battle cry whenever I heard what wasn't possible. Because of my young age. Because of my boys. Because I'd now chosen to be single and raise them. Because I couldn't find the small-sized place afforded to me as a mother, not quite large enough for me to breathe. Let's not forget the best of them all; because I am a woman.

"Watch me," I whispered. Shoulders back, chin up.

Working two paid jobs, juggling lectures, caring for a long-term sick son with an autoimmune illness, caring for three other rowdy sons, essay writing, co-parenting, dating and, I'll level with you, growing up alongside the boys as they grew too. I'd answer the door to salesmen who'd ask, "is yer Mam in?". By this time, she'd given up on my ludicrous ideas, well above my station. And yes, this Mam was in.

"Watch me," I grimaced. Back straight, firm smile.

Winging a first degree, perfecting essay writing through the night, funding a tiny house, school uniforms, car and child care in a hotchpotch logistical maze of cards, ever likely to fall with some unexpected blip of a bill, high temperature or accidental over-sleep-in. Learning who and what to trust, leaning into sisterhood and leaving behind ideas that life could if at all, be handed to me on a plate were all lessons – cold, loving and raw ones. Lashings of graft and discipline etched themselves into my days. I needed to believe what I put in would be mirrored by what I'd get out.

"Watch me," I held my breath, stomach tight.

Bright-eyed with another degree in the making and a belly full of another baby, I prepared to welcome my fifth son. The odds were off for a daughter. The juxtaposition of business school studies laced with feminist analyses while growing penises didn't escape me. In passing, I mention to the department head that I'll be absent for a fortnight and he asks the holiday destination. It's not like we don't see one another regularly, but my impending birth comes as a surprise. It's a close-knit post-grad family; everyone an HR professional ('cept me) decades older so this peachy addition to the group is a big event.

"Watch me," pushed through induced hell.

It takes the midwives' repeated unfolding of the layers around the baby to convince me this isn't a boy. I'm adamant they've got it wrong. More taking apart the tiny swaddle for me to check and put them right. Unswaddle. Argue. Repeat. Never beyond initial seconds of a maybe did it land in my mind that I'd be a mother of anything other than sons. No attachment, mere fact. There are some things that don't happen to me, like growing taller than five feet or leaving the house without making my bed, and this was one of them; I'm not the mother of a daughter.

"Watch me," as I wept joy. Boobs out, eyes on academic prize.

At my PhD scholarship panel, I'm asked, "hypothetically, how do you think children will affect your performance as a scholar when you have them?". Shifting one buttock to the other, I can't decide whether to bust their fuckwittery right there, and blast my chances to smithereens or answer this unholy illegality with a limp platitude. Locking my gaze with the questioner, I cut it at, "I'm confident in myself" and sit through the eerie silence that follows.

"Watch me," I middle fingered. Jaw locked.

THE NOISE SAYS
MOTHERHOOD IS
OUR CALLING

The Noise says being a mother is the be-all and end-all of a woman's life. Motherhood sits on a pedestal above everything we choose to do. The persistent notion is that childbearing somehow represents the goal and *culmination point* of a woman's existence. Some women are afforded a currency inextricably linked to childbearing and motherhood; others are not. As a white middle-class woman, my use to society is queried unless I'm a mother. Being a mother is a given as a life course, I'm told. I've pretty much always been a mother, so this Noise hasn't pestered or got to me. But that doesn't mean to say I'm unaware of the tattle that does affect me, and that simply won't desist.

To be a mother is both everything and simultaneously nothing. It's to undertake the hardest, unpaid labour of love that exists, yet there's something that's nagged at me for years as I watch the way mothers are held high yet treated as worthless. We're both pedestaled and revered as the moral compass of the world (as custodians of future generations' morals) while simultaneously cast as down-trodden supporters. It is equally the most important and least recognised job in the world. A head-fuck, if ever there was one.

To be a mother is to inadvertently claim a principal identity in life though this isn't obvious because it seems so 'right'. I question why, in toy stores, there are dollies, doll prams, doll clothes, and doll kits, but only in the aisles coloured pink. It'll be those toy prams or the adverts on television showing girls putting doll babies on potties, or simply playing mum, that contribute to teaching us our role. If these aren't powerful messages, why ever would toy brands bother with them? Modern motherhood is no longer viewed as simply a relationship with children, a role played at home and at school, or even an institution of sorts. Heather Havrilevsky puts it beautifully, *"motherhood has been elevated – or demoted – to the realm of a lifestyle, an all-encompassing identity with demands and expectations that eclipse everything else in life"*.

Allegedly, and as scary as any horror movie, motherhood completes a woman. In the 1970s, Anne Oakley argued in her ground-breaking research on housework that there exists in our culture an ideology that links women's identities to their role as mothers. But it was later in her semi-autobiographical account within *Taking it Like a Woman* (1984) that she states, *"the tension between the interests of the family and the interests of women as individuals has been rising for some two centuries. It is not possible for these interests to be reconciled".*

It's these 'irreconcilable' interests that cause immense Noise. Who is interested in the woman in her own right if not as the family's gentle, calm facilitator? Who cares that *"you might feel like the same person deep inside,…what the world apparently sees is a woman lugging around a giant umbilical cord".* Heather Havrilesky's words show how the woman's identity is submerged by the all-encompassing one of being a mother; once we're mothers, nothing matters as much as motherhood. Our primary way to experience self-realisation (apparently) lies in our maternity and alongside this, mother's abilities are not ultimately for ourselves, but for our children.

Mic Drop: This is not the case for men as fathers, but that's a whole different conversation for another time and another book.

Before we move onto mothers' abilities being solely for our children, let's ponder Turkey's president, Recep Tayyip Erdoğan, who during an International Women's Day speech in 2016, advised "*a woman is above all else a mother*" and that women without children are "*lacking*", "*deficient*" and "*half a person*". The general vibe is that being childless (not a word I like though let's keep this because that's what others use as a descriptor) is deviant. Not being a mother, involuntarily or by choice, brings on the need for justifications like "I'm just not maternal", "it never happened", or "one day, maybe". Motherhood oughtn't be an obligatory life path or perceived as the natural position women will take up. Having children is still seen as essential to being a woman, and if a woman doesn't, she's fallen from her true calling. One hundred percent bull, *agreed?!*

Back to our abilities as mothers then. The 'good mother' was described in the late 1990s as 'child-centred'. Mother-work represents what it means to be a mother and to experience what we call mothering. It's this type of mothering, as being the pinnacle of a woman's life, that interests me. While the phrase 'Intensive Mothering' was coined by Sharon Hays in the mid 1990s, it's easy to recognise the all-giving, all-present mothering in practice. Intensive Mothering appears to be a set of beliefs and assumptions about what it means to be a 'good mother', and it doesn't stop there. Behavioural and emotional aspects of childrearing are reflected from these beliefs. In other words, our ability to be a 'good' mother needs to be demonstrated by specific ways of raising our kids. *Listen to this crazy shit coming up!*

Peggy Orenstein called this 'the perfect mother', an idealised woman for whom childbearing surpasses all other identities. At the heart of this cheery, perfect mother ideal is her ability to give fully of herself, physically, emotionally, financially, psychologically and intellectually. It's impossible standards or Mother Stoppers that inform and remind us of the 'right' ways to mother. The focus is on the children, and all their concerns, as the only source of self-realisation and self-fulfilment for mothers. It's the children that become the *raison d'etre* for 'good and perfect' mothers.

This 'standard' of mothering police's *all* mothering and ends up being, what Andrea O'Reilly calls, *"the pathologizing of women who do not and cannot practice intensive mothering"*. Because violating this maternal norm through diverse parenting practices or forming alternative family compositions may constitute 'bad mothering', and lead to social and legal penalties (Jennifer Reich, 2014). Though often overlooked, interpretations of and approaches to 'good mothering' differ based on mothers' social contexts. White middle-class perspectives on intensive mothering bang home that the child should always be front and centre of mothers' lives, no matter what. Each child must grow up knowing the mother is the source of all their wishes. Because in treating children as people with desires and rights of their own, we've stopped treating ourselves and other mothers in the same vein. Note: by empowering the child did we *have* to disempower mothers?. In the perfect mother role, our purpose is to facilitate the lives of the children we create. Our lives, therefore, become a dedication to them and the disappearance of us as people in our own right is a given. I'm conscious that the Mother Stopping Noise of perfect mothering is often lived out as personal 'choices'. These are indeed choices made by individuals, but they're choices informed by narrow narratives of what being a 'good' mother really means. Cultural ideologies often work as a kind of road map for life choices, don't they?

Prior to the mid 19th century, work was largely home based, and women and men tended to share the rearing of children. Changes brought about by industrialisation took men away from homes as they transitioned into the public sphere of factory and office jobs. Mothers began to be viewed as a child's best caretaker. This idea grew out of the separation of public and private spheres that divided work and home, making home the domain of women and child rearing the responsibility of mothers. This 'cult of domesticity' occurred in white populations of means, largely excluding women of colour and working-class white women. These women had been working outside of the home in service jobs for generations. Any whitewashed chronology ignores the complexity of the Noise that's dominated mothers' lives. Angela Davis encapsulated this when she wrote that while Afro-American women and white women were subjected to multiple unwanted pregnancies and had to clandestinely abort, Afro-American women were also suffering from compulsory sterilisation programmes that were not discussed within reproductive justice dialogue.

The ongoing responsibility for perfect children, perfect house, and perfect family life are all part of women's individual choices', and not seen as part of systemic Mother Stopping cultures. IF a mother does not run her home smoothly, use her organising skills to deliver extracurricular sport, music and language lessons to her children, plan and host memorable birthday parties, and deliver tons of child-centred activities; she's failing her maternal responsibilities. The assumption is that she'll need to find solutions to the daunting task of balancing her public and private life, her home and career (if she has a career). In this landscape of competitive individualistic lifestyle, mothers who do not undertake paid work outside of the family need to defend why this might be the case. We're trapped in never-ending circles, making choices that might seem like they exist, but in many cases simply don't.

Perfect motherhood is not possible. Perfect mothering is impossible too. As I listened to the Noise of 'perfect motherhood', the risk became obvious: to be locked in a kind of prison, bound by the 'myths' of motherhood chasing after ridiculous, elusive goals. Part of this double bind is that whichever choice is chosen, it will be wrong. The Noise promulgating perfect mother standards stink. Two side effects of the stress-laden demands of contemporary good mothering are: 1. Internalisation of perceived inadequacies as personal failures, which can result in distress, insecurity, anxiety and even/often depression, and 2. The competitive professionalisation of mothering.

Frank Furedi talks about this professionalisation in his book *Paranoid Parenting* (2008). He describes it like this, "*even the most routine [parenting act], is analysed in minute detail, correlated with a negative or positive outcome, and endowed with far-reaching implications for child development*". As Judith Suissa warns, the scientisation of the parent-child relationship means being a mother is a job for which we must learn the science or risk reaping the downfall of our child/ren.

Being a good mother is to keep up with all the baby and child kits that help children develop appropriately. The rub is that the kit isn't simply functional and/or for entertainment, it now attends to children's emotional needs, sensory developments, I.Q, and tech dexterity and skills. As Heather Havrilesky says, "*it used to be good enough just to keep your house from being coated in a thin layer of dog hair and human faeces"*, now mothers must be fully informed of the latest scientific research to meet the standard of being a 'good' mother. But it isn't really anything to do with the mother herself, it's all about her ability to shape a perfectly developed citizen to take up his/her/their useful place in society. The mother is only of interest in relation to her role as the facilitator of this citizen.

Jennifer Senior makes the point that there's an "enduring link" between women's increased independence and the cultural pressure for women to be "more attentive" in their mothering. The high stakes of women's independence translates into messages that every little choice a mother makes might result in drastic consequences in their children's. Let your baby cry itself to sleep? Your child might need therapy for attachment issues, and adulthood dysfunctional behaviour could well be laid at your metaphorical door. Breastfed your baby until they were four years old? Your child might need support for separation problems, and adulthood dysfunctional behaviour could well be laid at your metaphorical door. I use these as topical examples, not as weapons to use against mothers. Essentially: **What was it that you didn't or did do in your mothering to bring about your child's 'lack'?**

I could list pages and pages of speculative scenarios that could ultimately be seen as an inadequacy of the mother and her mothering: a lack, an overbearingness, a failure, multiple failures. The vastness of the responsibilities (in every way you can imagine) in mothering means the demands and judgements on mothers have vastly increased too. The jeopardy of motherhood exponentially exploded at a time when it's touted that women are more liberated. And it's a decent query to consider whether the professionalisation of mothering is designed to push (some) women back into the domestic where gender normative roles insist she belongs.

Of course, not all mothers are tugged back to the domestic. Certain kinds of motherhood, for example, single motherhood, immigrant motherhood, and welfare motherhood are marked and therefore seen differently. We know the intensive mothering ideology represents, as Tiffany Taylor says, "a *hegemonic form of mothering*". It dominates cultural understandings and descriptions, and obscures subcultural differences and inequalities in the material conditions under which mothering occurs.

Motherhood as a calling and a marker of triumphant femininity is not a homogenous concept. Race, education, and class all play a part too. White working-class mothers may well lean into motherhood as a calling when other options aren't as apparent or don't exist. Some mothers see motherhood as 'saving' them. It's documented that Black mothers talk of *raising* a child, whereas white mothers focus on *having* a child. In a large-scale study (Tichenor et al, 2016) on variations of attitudes toward being a mother by race, ethnicity and education, researchers found that Black mothers have a clearer distinction between having a child and raising a child, perhaps because of the cultural value of community mothering. This valuing of communal mothering has not been central to the ideology of Intensive Mothering and is in some opposition to Westernised ideals of motherhood as a calling. Asian women, for instance, are stereotyped as being successful in the world of work and, unlike Black and Hispanic women, haven't been labelled as hyper-fertile and/or welfare reliant. Within Indigenous worldviews, Tatjana Takševa advises *"producing life and raising children are understood as the creation of a people, a nation and a future – a sacred and highly valued social responsibility that Indigenous mothers are given the authority to exercise"*. Far from being women's individual annihilation, motherhood is perceived as an assertion of leadership and authority linked to life-giving and community building. Childcare is understood as both an individual and a social responsibility for Indigenous communities. As Tatjana Takševa mentions, women sometimes *"choose not to have biological children so they can better fulfil their roles of aunties or grannies or serve the community"*.

White middle-class mothers, like me, are torn between a calling of being the good and perfect mother, and a calling as the educated self-actualised worker. Considering motherhood as a calling through different race, education and class lenses is important, as there's a merging of factors that impact the experience of motherhood within different structural constraints across specific locations. Understanding the differences and intersections these locations create for mothers is key to the true intersectionality of the motherhood experience. I wonder how social policy would be different if we had a further understanding other than this intensive whitewashed mothering Noise. How might the Noise surrounding motherhood as a calling be different, if non-intensive mothering was embraced in its complexity and without hierarchy? The Noise about motherhood as the true calling of women affects *all* mothers and upholding intensive mothering as an ideal intensifies it even more.

As an example, let's look at the nuance of 'good' mothering for women with disabilities. Rebekah Taussig explains that "*disability expands into every possible corner and intersects with every other identity*". Claudia Malacrida also details how women with disabilities go to creative and extraordinary lengths to comply with ideal motherhood, perhaps as a way to lay claim to a maternal and sexual identity that society frequently denies them. Mothers with disabilities face enhanced challenges in achieving idealised mothering on the one hand, and they are particularly vulnerable to mother-blame and heightened scrutiny on the other. This is partly because women with disabilities often engage in mothering with fewer resources and more barriers in the public and private spheres than women without disabilities. Disabled women's mothering is often constrained by poverty, inadequate housing, and the inaccessibility of public spaces (Grue and Laerum, 2002). In addition to barriers in the economy and the built environment, mothers with disabilities face stigmatising public perceptions of them as inadequate or inappropriate in the role of mothering. Meanwhile, some disabled mothers acknowledge that being pregnant and engaging in motherhood is empowering precisely because, for the first time in their lives, they're seen as fully functioning adult women. As Claudia Malacrida says, *"intensive mothering and its performance instead provides these women with a positive self-image and acts as a route into normative femininity".*

Let me be blunter. I'm a white middle-class woman, used to the incessant Noise that motherhood is my highest calling. I was taught that being a good mother involves fitting into the model of intensive all-in mothering. And my biggest angst (apart from paying the bills as a single mother) is the stretch and ambivalence between my career and my kids. But all these challenges, I've been told, can be overcome.

Pure grit, hard work, and purpose-driven inner work; these are part of the solution for balancing my public and private spheres, career and family. The Noise also says that if other mothers can't make it all work and get careers going while raising kids, that's 'on them'. This is the easy but heinous explanation that avoids recognition of structural inequalities etched into our society. Unless, and until, I acknowledge these differences, I'll collude with and contribute to this harmful Noise, and it will never end.

Mother Stopper Culture and You

The nuance that exists within Mother Stopper cultures – and the variants of Mother Stoppers as a result – need to be explored on an individual level. I'd like to go back to Anne Oakley's sentiment that the interests of the family are always in competition with the interests of women as individuals.

Let's unpack that a little:

1. "It is not possible for these interests to be reconciled" is what Anne Oakley claims, so how are your own deep interests currently not being reconciled within your family home? Or maybe they <u>are</u> being reconciled. If so, how?
2. If not reconciled, what Noise is driving you away from reconciling your interests with those of your family?

3. What versions of 'good motherhood' show up in your life and how do you hold yourself accountable to these ideals?
4. Where did you learn these versions and what Noise reinforces them?
5. What intersections of Mother Stopper culture are present in your life?

If I had a pound for every time strangers said, "you know what causes that, right?", "same husband?" or "you've got your hands full!" – I'd have enough to buy a small yacht. People smirked or winked as if we shared an in-joke about my [supposedly] incompetent contraception. My uterus, my vagina, and their visitors were consistently up for public comment, everywhere and all the time. In supermarkets as I bought cans of tuna and bags of cat litter. As I stood in a school shoe shop queue, ticket in hand. In GP rooms with sore throats, head lice and verrucas. A resolution to this 'problem' was needed.

So, I sorted it.

After my sterilisation, I remarried, published prolifically, and was refused one Professorship because I was 'too glossy'. Everlasting thanks to the Russell Group HR director who called me in indignation at the result and spilled the discriminatory beans while telling me, "I'll be fired if you push back on the uni's decision". Not to be thwarted, I wore a sludge brown skirt suit for my next professorial interview but, of course, all I was really doing was hiding myself. There was also the very real fact that I was the solo female of childbearing age in competition with three white, bald academics, some twenty plus years older than myself.

In the 'too glossy' feedback I was told my publications were the best, but that I was a bit of a media gal (a risk), a woman with a future (there's time for you, we'll employ an older man), and I might have other distractions (you'll leave to have a baby). It was excruciating to get in front of interview panels only to be pipped to the post by white, pale, and ~~possibly~~ definitely stale compatriots in my field.

I didn't have the luxury to linger over years of gentle productivity. I behaved like a mother academic: I had a job to be done, less time than needed to do it and high hopes for myself and my five children. Who were all more than fine, they were thriving. The momentous decision to reverse my sterilisation hit me like a ton of nuns. My husband and I didn't assume the microsurgery would work; hallelujah, a year from that surgery, I held a miracle second daughter in my arms after the first maternity leave of my life. During which I wrote loads, became an online agony aunt, and set up my own consulting firm. It was less sofa time, more multi kinds of birthing.

As an army family, we'd moved again. My tenured university role was now more than five hours away on the train. At the height of my academic career curve, I felt tested, stretched taut, and oddly exhilarated. The obvious response to all this was to surrender my post and ramp back in favour of an easier traditional life. Supporting my husband's career while accepting that my own (though parallel in money and status) would have to become less, was expected. That age-old compromise of having children was pressuring me to put paid to what I'd worked hard for. And it didn't make it less choke worthy knowing it was a well-worn solution enacted by many.

I committed to not be beaten by the structures that have been holding women back for decades and stayed in my role. That's when I discovered, on adding my husband to the account I'd held for some fifteen years, my bank no longer placed me as the primary account holder. Being a man elevated him above me, it seemed. In discussion with the bank, I was told it wasn't personal, "it's the way the system's built". Then I walked into an academic dinner event to hear a male colleague telling the table, "she's only so senior because she's slept her way into the post". Pulling up my chair, I sat down amongst them. All I could feel was a thrilling sense of livid revolution. This man couldn't have been more wrong. Oddly, he didn't continue by confiding about the many ways he'd cornered me physically, and all the kind yet firm refusals I'd given him. Me, lips to the microphone: "In my defence, I really love a good buffoon joke, your honour."

Make no mistake. I was gobsmacked when baby number seven was on her way. I'd won a lottery in being blessed. It was effortless to name this little one: Madeline – tower, elevated, and magnificent. Growing her and my ability to straddle the demands of all the kids' different ages wasn't as tough as navigating conversations about *why I still insisted on working. I was getting tired of justifying myself.*

The phrase "I hope it's worth it" caused a guttural reaction that made me want to upchuck down my blouse every time a snarky (well-meaning) person made a comment about my working life. But all that stopped when I discovered Madeline was dead in my womb. For no reason, (the post mortem results showed months later), her heart simply stopped. Days later, once my husband could return from a Scottish peak expedition, I birthed her perfect body. She was magnificent in the tiny basket midwives laid her to rest in. Scattering her ashes across the hills, I had to become a stronger woman.

THE NOISE SAYS MOTHERS
MUST BE SELFLESS

In general, women are socialised to be other-directed; to be concerned with the feelings of others and likewise to be conscious of, and seek approval from, others. When a woman becomes a mother, a significant change happens beyond the obvious inclusion of a child. The shift from (seemingly) self-determined individual to mother is not an exact or precise process. Nevertheless, by the time a child is born, the mother will realise through external Noise, that her needs are relegated to a lower status than those of her child.

I could never truly understand this because, in my case, the fact I became a mother at such an early age meant I didn't have time for being ME in the linear way motherhood tends to be presented (in some circles). Neither had I given it thought, in any significant way, about how my own mother and her needs ~~might~~ were relegated beneath and behind mine. The reason this is worth writing explicitly about is that: 1. Because of my own internalised version of what it takes to be a good mother, I'd always ignored my own mother's needs. I didn't query this until some years later, and 2. I wasn't exposed to the interior experience of being a 'self-determined individual' for any length of time. I went from being a teenage child to a teenage mother.

The skipping of an assumed stage (from a white middle-class perspective) left me relying immediately on external Noise about what it means to be a 'good' mother. While my peers were studying for A-levels, I was tending cracked nipples and mastitis. Later, I learned they were working or at university. I had zero peers to check out mother-norms with: I was the outlier.

Meanwhile, I consumed every book I could possibly get my hands on from the library about motherhood and raising happy children. I talked with mothers who birthed at the same time(s) as me (all older than myself). I was searching for ways to grow into being me and for my children to grow into them too. I was looking for a win-win of sorts, and with this, I had to look at what it now means to *be* a child.

We can trace through the history of child-hood to see how it's become a narration of liberation. It's a narrative that blanket positions children in the past as servants, or apprentices, and that their lives were regimented. In this version, if you were female, you spent your childhood spinning thread or doing menial chores, and if you were a boy, you worked in a factory or a shop.

It's generally agreed how much better off kids are today, but Steven Mintz suggests it's a more complicated and ambivalent story. It's important to recognise that childhood is never unambiguous or homogeneously constructed <u>and</u> it has never been so. Most childhoods are built up with internal contradictions and con-flicting messages. The transition from child labour to compulsory schooling and a higher leaving age created a whole new childhood. This meant a change in the very meaning of child-hood and the demands on mothers increased since they were expected to send clean, healthy children to school. Fast forward to this new version; a non-useful child, dependent on a breadwinning father and a caring mother. A new emotionality in the family – the caring element – was also now a part of this.

Additionally, a new 'normal' was established. It was essential for everyone to benefit from what was considered the blessings of youth. At the same time, a new view of the family was created, with new roles for all members, not least children. This new normality, which doesn't always agree with reality but which could at least be measured against it, emerged.

Being a child now is not just a matter of being and existing. It's transformed into life's great project, and the outline of today's childhood includes: early maturity, sharing the experiences of the adult world through social media and mass media, and quickly learning adult behaviour and the codes that apply in the adult world by participating in institutions outside the home. It's a childhood full of demands for achievement and expectations, but if children are to succeed they must begin early (read:

engage in all those prenatal and postnatal scientised activities). We can also track how working life has been postponed and how taking part in work is seen as unsuitable for children. Ironically, this is at the same time schools bridge the gap between school and work via work experience programmes. The transition from child labour to pocket money is symbolic of the changed role of children. What is the significance and agenda behind pocket money? As a symbol of family membership, or reward for making beds, washing up and more? Is pocket money educational for children to learn how to handle money? All, partial or none of this? Is it a symbol of maturity for children, who otherwise have to wait to the age of god-knows-when before they get their first job – the traditional symbol of adulthood? Our inner child's states as well as their outer world activities are typically mother-structured, mother-supervised and for the mother to be sensitive to.

Let me tell you about my dear friend Rose. After years of trying to conceive, she was elated to learn she was pregnant. At last, she'd enjoy what she'd seen so many of us experience. She was brim-full of questions – practical, spiritual, financial – all through her feminist lens. One big question she asked me was: *How can a mother not want to give her everything to her child, including herself?* Casting aside a gender reveal party, she wed herself to raising her child on gender-neutral terms. Absorbing ideas on how to do this dominated her days when she started mentioning night time leg pains. Her midwife told her to not worry. So, she didn't. During the birth, it became apparent all wasn't as it ought to be. The baby was healthy and safe, but Rose wasn't. In the months that followed, she got used to being a mother at the same time as grappling with late-stage cancer. Her big question changed to: *How can we thrive as mothers without over giving until depletion or annihilation?* She asked if it was necessary to give herself over to motherhood and if this was expected. Rose's struggle for life was stark. Just before her death, she mentioned what she called an existential crisis and challenge deeply embedded in mothering. Does it have to be a choice between my baby or me getting what we need?

We care and fight for children's welfare and children's rights, but when is this done for mothers? We don't care, for instance, if a mother is happy, not in herself. Interest in mothers is in relation to the child (their continuing welfare, their needs) so questions revolve around, "Are you depressed?", "Are you any danger to the child?" not, "Are you alright yourself?" – unattached from utility, family productivity and labour. As Aurelie Athan recounts, *"currently and historically, most research related to motherhood isn't actually about the mother. It's usually about her impact on her children…how her choices, health, wellbeing and life impacts her child's experience. We rarely reflect on the mother's subjective experience. Many times, in studies her behaviour is observed or measured, but we don't directly ask about her feelings. We might study things like a mother's folic acid intake but only on how it improves her child's cognitive abilities, not how it benefits her".*

Research and interests in mothers are related

to her ability to perform in her role as a mother, not her role as a *human* who is a mother. Aurelie Athan makes the point that mothers are studied through a pathology lens – when something's wrong – or *"when they are mad or they've gone mad. We only pay attention to women's experiences at their most distressful"*. If we accept that interest in mothers isn't about us per se, but about our children (other than the caveat of interest in mothers who don't fit or can never fit such as mothers without racial, economic and marital privilege) then we begin to see how as Andrea O'Reilly puts it, *"the ideology of mothering is defined by the belief that good mothering entails selfless and unconditional love for one's child/ren"*.

The Noise about motherhood revolves around the central principle that mothers must deliver unconditional love. The presence of this unconditional love isn't explicitly spoken about, although recognition around postpartum depression shows that the immediacy of an outpouring of love for a baby can, and often does, take time. The connection between mother and baby, in the context of postnatal mental health turbulence and disorders, is questioned. BUT, unless these are present, it's taken as given that unconditional love just simply happens for 'good mothers'. Unconditional love is at the heart of our motherhood model (and being the 'good and perfect' mother). It's the unspoken pact that a mother will love her child/ren, no matter what. That she will benefit the child/ren at the cost of herself because the Noise says that kids who are loved unconditionally thrive; everything else is inconsequential by comparison. Of course, that unconditional love is independent of reciprocity because, *"if you describe something as unconditional, you mean that the person doing or giving it does not require anything to be done by other people in exchange"* and it's *"without conditions or limitations". (Collins Dictionary, 2018).*

Unconditional love is a practice demonstrated by the constant action of being selfless, which some even suggest is synonymous with femininity itself (pass the vomit bowl). In the centre of motherhood, the unswerving principle is this gospel-like implicit contract of a sacrifice of self to raise our child/ren. Internalised Noise of exacting standards on 'good mothering' keeps us tethered to selflessness. The basis of this is that if we love our children unconditionally, we will voluntarily want to sacrifice who we are because that is the way we show we love them. We love them through this activity called 'being selfless'. Therefore, we need to continue selflessness to continue proving the extent to which we love our children.

This double bind means that when a mother says, "I have needs of my own," she's seen as selfish. To be self-centric is transgressive. For mothers to attend to their/our own needs and to place these as important (let alone first) in life is not only taboo but essentially a game-changer. It's arresting to unpack as it de-stabilises ideas of motherhood, love, and essentialist notions of what it is to be female. Many mothers equate 'good' mothering with self-sacrifice.

Let's take something as simple as greetings cards. You'll know the kind – Mother's Day ones are especially good for us to think about here. Shonda Rhimes was surprised about the following, "*I don't think it ever occurred to me before how much and how often women are praised for displaying traits that basically render them invisible. When I really think about it, I realise the culprit is the language generally used to praise women*".

Here are some of the sentiments in these cards celebrating mothers:

- ◇ *She sacrificed everything for her children.*
- ◇ *She never thought about herself.*
- ◇ *She gave up everything for us.*
- ◇ *She worked tirelessly to make sure we had what we needed.*
- ◇ *She stood in the shadows, she was the wind beneath our wings.*

These words exemplify what mothers are rewarded for; sacrifice, being selfless, giving up everything for others, and working the self to near disappearance. As Shonda Rhimes continues, "*it's good how Mom diminishes and martyrs herself. The message is: mothers, you are such wonderful and good people because you make yourselves smaller, because you deny your own needs, because you toil tirelessly in the shadows and no one ever thanks or notices you... this all makes you AMAZING"*.

The motherhood pendulum swung some time ago into a role expecting us to provide, serve and grow future generations in an intensive sacrificial mode all set within the banal euphoria of family life. The traits held high for mothers to rise to are laden with diminishments – doer for others and all giving workhorse. It seems fitting that the clergy during the 1500s would tell women as they were preparing to give birth, that they were preparing to die. Modern motherhood brings a different kind of decaying of self yet it's unsurprising that Meg Conley describes selfless motherhood as, *"the steel frame that holds up a prosperous society"*.

To be taught, through Noise, that mothers are the lynchpin upon which the home and all relationships depend is antithetical to our own self-fulfilment. Or does self-fulfilment apply to everyone else, except mothers? No, seriously. But without the answer I want, Mary Oliver shakes us down tenderly with her on-point question, *"when will you have a little pity for every soft thing that walks through the world, yourself included?"*

Enter: the desperate need for self-care, AKA yoga, candles, tampons made of soy, and about 300 Tibetan prayers. (Thanks to Ash Ambirge for this side stage plea).

Which brings up the topic of self-care as an antidote because mothers are allowed a tiny injection of self-care, in service of keeping going: *Have that wine, my love. You run that bubble bath. Pop and have your nails done. Maybe even have a spa day. But don't run away with yourself.* Self-care, that trivialised idea that seems to follow two patterns: 1. Good mothers sacrifice themselves, or 2. Good mothers also practice self-care to accomplish good mothering. While many mothers try to balance self-sacrifice and self-care, most of us talk about self-care and self-sacrifice as mutually exclusive elements of good mothering. As much as self-care might be beneficial, how we define it and whether we practice it fluctuates. Is self-care necessary for good mothering, and if so, how do we incorporate it into our lives? For some, it's a non-negotiable element of mothering. Race, class, and family structure also undoubtedly influence mothers' views and practices of self-care.

Is self-care a luxury? Is a career *part of* self-care? Do the co-existence of self-sacrifice and self-care practices of mothering <u>cause</u> conflict and need for an apology because mothers need or (god forbid) want to invest in ourselves? Does self-care become legitimate when linked to serving and caring for other people? Bad mothers would be those who love themselves more than they love their children, *right?!* The many meanings of this, make it hard to know when a mother crosses the line of self-serving rather than other-serving. Equally, a bad mother might not practice self-care because she just doesn't realise she ought to in order to care for other people better. Whether we're fiercely guarding self-care or letting it slip to the end of our priorities, it seems self-care might just be a site of resistance. Then again maybe, as Audre

Lorde says, *"caring for myself is not self-indulgence, it is self-preservation, and that is an act of political warfare"*.

Reconciling the tension between self-care as luxury and necessity depends on economic and marital privilege. The time and/or resources needed to practice self-care must be afforded. Mother-centric self-care cannot always be enacted in families where child-centric activities are needed to build social capital and access future opportunities. For example, as Evette Dionne tells us, *"ordinarily, particularly for Black women, we don't have time to take care of ourselves. Many of us are poor, many of us are working ourselves into graves, early graves particularly, and many of us put everybody before ourselves. So, standing and saying that I matter and that I'm important and that taking care of myself is important is a radical act because so often, we're expected to take care of everybody else, that we're supposed to come last, almost as if it's a familial expectation"*.

How challenging is it, then, for Black women to exact self-care? Self-care may be a buzz-phrase these days, but the race, gender, and class dynamics behind the concept are often not discussed. For white women of means, self-care is the 'acceptable face of being your own person once a mother' (bubble baths, alcohol, retail therapy, wild swimming, personal grooming). Some mothers can eke out pockets of 'self-care' to fulfil their life's role; servicing and serving children and their partner/husband.

After all, as Eleanor Brown sums up nicely, *"we can't make a difference in the world unless we are giving from a place of fullness in ourselves".* As much as this is progress in recognising women (mothers) can't live from depletion, the implicit message is that giving rather than being is the aim. Remember, for Black women self-care is a radical act as Evette Dionne argues, *"because we've spent generations in servitude to others. In fact, Black women have often been considered properties of our communities".*

Self-care may be both a revolutionary act <u>and</u> an upholding of the status quo of serving others, but this depends on the myriad of social locations of women. Women of colour have unique perspectives on self-care from white women. Poor women have unique perspectives on self-care from middle-class women. Single mothers have unique perspectives from married mothers. And so on.

Nevertheless, a lot of people are going to tell *all* mothers that it's our choice. When we choose to have children, we choose to take on caregiving. We insist on taking responsibility for frivolous things like feeding people at regular intervals and basic personal and home hygiene, so of course, we can't have lives of our own. Except there are plenty of fathers who continue their lives as before.

It's all supposed to stop when we become mothers: our dreams, our desires, our existence as people. We're told repeatedly, by bosses, friends, family and by ourselves, from nearly every corner of our culture, that all that must stop once we become mothers. Self-care is admissible if it allows us to keep tamed, acquiesced and agile in our abilities to be selfless or as I prefer to call it, less of ourselves.

The Unconditional Act of Selfless Self-Care

I've attempted to unpack this ideology of unconditional love that mothers are supposed to imbue into every part of our lives, again, conscious of the fact that 'unconditional' is conditional to the version of motherhood and Mother Stopper cultures that are systemic in your life. As are, the ways we are 'allowed' to practice self-care.

Both these ideologies – of being unconditional and self-care – are tightly packed with the broader notion of being the 'good and perfect' mother. The Noise is very clear on the 'right' ways we go about both.

So, let's look at that:

1. What does 'unconditional love' look like in your version of motherhood?
2. How are your ideas of being 'unconditional' or selfless with your children shaped by the Noise in your life?
3. What does 'good and perfect' mothering mean to you?
4. What does bad mothering mean to you?

5. In what ways are you 'allowed' to practice self-care (according to the Mother Stopper cultures that exist) in your version of motherhood?

6. In what ways are your self-care needs left unaddressed because of this?

Before we move forward, *let's* talk about the time I 'had' a house husband.

Before I was a career woman, my husband and I decided we'd reshuffle roles from his as breadwinner and me as baby-making supremo and homemaker. It felt right until it didn't, so we chose to change things up. A few months into me forging out from the home, I returned from work to find something I'd not considered.

My husband in his dressing gown. The home in chaos.

I stood lipsticked in a black pencil skirt, all revved up from a day making waves, crestfallen. There was expressed breast milk caked on his shoulder and a faint smell of unwashed teeth as he laid the table for our supper. This once strong-shouldered man stooped. He held himself as less-than-before even though he was (mostly) enjoying caring for our kids. Finding time to do perfunctory personal admin tasks (showering, *clipping toenails, even eating) were proving quite the challenge.*

And there was me out in the world, finally. Making my mark. Finding my voice. Rising up that little bit. The contrast was stark and unexpected.

I knew the daily grind of kids and their relent- less dress-feed-bathe-undress-feed routine. Plus, the tidy-wash-up-tidy-play-tidy cycle of never- ending insanity-making stuff. It had messed with my head, grappling my confidence to the ground. I knew that place well. But I hadn't expected my beloved lifelong career-man husband to buckle with such speed. I thought his backlogged decades in work would be some kind of buffer for at least a year or two before he showed signs of the erosion of himself.

The disappearance of self in raising kids can be a slow, gradual loss. Or it can be a kaboom style, overnight leakage of who we are. What I hadn't anticipated (in fact, I'd banked on his years of solid gold weighted selfhood as a working man) was that my husband didn't know who he was without his work identity. His merging into our

*children was sudden. His disappearance to himself,
speedy, precisely because the very idea of who he
was and what his purpose was in the world was
tightly wrapped up in the external world of work.
Not in intensive fathering. Not in the unending
repetition of raising kids. Instead, when he stepped
out of productivity and into domesticity, he was
cut astray from all he knew, including himself.*

*This taught me something that I was too
ensnared in before to fully recognise; being ourselves and growing who we are while raising kids
is a radical act requiring conscious effort. What
that means practically is that we must invest
thought, time, energy, love, compassion and
care into ourselves, separate from our families.
We must give oxygen to our souls' desires and to
the spirit we grew in ourselves before we became
mothers. The person we are is more than mother.
And father.*

---

*It's over. It's the first weekend after the summer
holidays end. Done and busted open. Another*

fantasy-summer-together laid to rest. Dead till it comes around next year.

For them: Lazy, fun, adventures. Sunshine, movies, outings. Relaxed, play, treats. Long days, makeshift dens, meals with pudding. Routine interrupted. Soft shoes, shorts, squabbles. Lazy, fun adventures.

Last year we wild camped with friends Swallows and Amazon style. Nothing posh, beans out of a can yet pure gold to take us through the dank winter. But it set me up for failure. Because this year I went laissez-faire. Off-piste. In other words, I winged it. This is from a woman who plans detail meticulously. How else do you imagine I keep so much together? Work, family, sanity, and of course, peace of mind.

Back to the summer, though. I was less prepared than my usual curated logistical puzzle. As a result, I was less prepared for the feeling of being sucked into a summer world, sharply reduced. I'd forgotten what it was to have what I'd known as my life suddenly dissolve, right in front of my own eyes. What's worse, it was all by my own making.

Only weeks before, I'd been an orb of

productivity, a lightning rod for action and razor focus. But everything changed when my teens stopped their exams following close on the back of months of revision meltdowns and a merry-go-round hormonal thrill ride. Within days I was searching for my former working self but couldn't find her. Although I could just about glimpse myself, in snatched pockets of time at the edge of everything family, I felt emptied against my own will. I knew – but had forgotten in naive amnesia – that unless I insist wholeheartedly on myself in a manner of life and deathlike advocacy, then I will have to check my own life at the door.

Let's burst the bubble that my kids' lives are mine. That their concerns, interests and adventures are entangled mirrors of mine. Naturally, I want my children to revel in life, to take their pleasure with it and to never tire of excavating meaning from all they put into it. But they are NOT me. I am separate from them. It beggars belief that I feel it's necessary to speak this obvious delineation. They are them, I am me.

When they, for instance, have lengthy holidays it's assumed (in many circles) that I'll vacate *myself enough to concentrate on those I say I love. Caregiving is a fucking extreme deal. As systems stand – educationally, organisationally, financially, governmentally, societally – mothers' lives are not our own. They belong to our children. Their lives belong to them, as a right. Our lives, if we're mothers, belong to our children too. As a right. *steps off my soapbox**

This summer (because I shoehorned myself around the needs of others) I've stretched myself to near oblivion. When I had discussed with one teen about team playing, pulling together and my own need to find time to think, I was met with the classic, "you chose to have us, don't be a mother if you don't want to focus just on us".

To collide full frontal with a cage-making narrative of motherhood spewed from my own sweet child must go down as nothing short of a travesty. What I know is that when I chose to become a mother, I did not also subscribe to an annihilation of my own self. Some compromise, sure. Death of myself, no thanks. But this summer I forgot to battle plan for myself. I forgot to create my personal war room so that I could decide on 'military' tactics to hold onto myself. I got complacent because I thought, after so many summers as a mother, I knew the ropes. I couldn't have been more wrong. I fell foul of the notion that I'd been here before when in reality I've not. Not with these children, and not in these specific circumstances.

As they enter the autumn term (talking fondly of summer memories) and face fresh futures, I'm left knowing I was outmanoeuvred by systems that don't give a damn about what I, as a person in my own right, want and need.

My role as mum trumps my role as a person. This summer I couldn't figure in the centre of my own life because I didn't make sure that I could. No one, least of all my family, will make this happen, on my behalf. In a world that teaches women that once we become mothers, it's all about others, my job is to commit to myself more than leaning into any spoon-fed mumsy fantasy laced with self-harming naïveté that'll surely undo me.

Next year's summer holiday must be different.

THE NOISE SAYS MOTHERS
MUST MAKE OUR
CHILDREN HAPPY

The messages to women, especially mothers, are that it's dangerous to try to do too much, be too much, and to 'bite off more than can be chewed' because there'll be *consequences*. These messages span the demise of hetero-relationships (on the basis that some men perceive they are being asked to play second fiddle to a career and/or child), our own health (burnout) and most importantly, our children's welfare, health and attainment, which in turn might affect our children's future employment and chances in life.

Rules must be followed, but not a definitive set of rules laid out for us, of course. That's naive to imagine or deliver. It's a differentiated set of rules that alter depending on our structural location, but compliance of some kind is required. Building on the Good Girl Model put forward by Kasia Urbaniak, where people-pleasing women are rewarded, and those challenging good girl rules are punished, mothers are meant to excel at being 'good'. As Celia Dodd critiqued, *"if women don't follow the rules, they risk damaging not only their children's health but that of future generations"*. We are, after all, seen as the conscience of the world and the future of humanity rests on our shoulders.

Exacting 'good and perfect' mother model standards, heaped upon us, play out so that, *"if you're a good mother, your kid will go to Harvard; if you're a bad mother, your kid will be an axe murderer,"* as Susan Douglas and Meredith Michaels say; summing up society's unquestioning belief in a mother's accountability. From this stance, it's possible to see the paradigm that believes you can do *A* and *B* to produce a child like *C*, a suspicious twentieth-century development with roots in the 1920s, when childrearing advice exploded. With the rise of psychology, parenting experts (read: male) weighed in on mothers' behaviours and decisions, and how they affected their children (often adversely).

For starters, 'amateur' mothers weren't

believed to be trusted voices of wisdom. Secondly, in making parenting such a daunting job for which women's intuition couldn't be relied on, and for which male experts had to be consulted, women were pulled back toward prescribed gender roles (Jennifer Senior, 2014).

The point is that the Noise implies mothers, <u>not parents</u>, are the sole determinants of our children's health, wellbeing and success. One post-war theory – Attachment Parenting – suggested that a child's emotional bond with its parents has lasting consequences. It's curious to consider when and why the bond with fathers has been relegated as less critical than that of a mother. Despite the positive impact of feminism, men have an unquestionable option to make their career their child. The legitimate role of a man's earning potential is often used as a way to explain absentee fathering. The practice of saying 'parenting', when really the activity is one mothers are expected to perform, continues. Attachment parenting is not 'co-attachment' for the responsibility of the child/ren – it speaks to mothering as generously including the other parent, but where this is a father, it allows him to not truly be accountable. This might be different if the default role of a woman was not that of being a mother.

Throughout my years as a mother, I've always been assumed to be 'in charge' and 'lead parent' in my children's overall wellbeing. This includes emotional welfare, the planning of and attending to what makes them happy, as well as their physical health. That's not to say I've been single the entire time of my motherhood. It's more to highlight the everyday practice and response-ability, or ability to respond, has been mine regardless of how progressive my partner or husband has been. The task of shaping a functional, contributing, emotionally-stable and happy citizen is given to mothers. This might seem natural to you, but why exactly are mothers allocated accountability for this monumental task?

If 'good' motherhood rules aren't followed, we run the risk of raising fucked up children. Comply with the role of the 'good and perfect' mother and you may, *just may*, get the reward of a well-rounded child/adult. The Mother Stopping Noise would even have us believe the more self we pour into our children, the more likely we will achieve this ideal result. Plus, if we adhere to the *'do A and B to produce a child like C'* approach, a lasting, loving relationship will develop with these wonderful children, who will also be thankful for all that's been done for them.

Let's take a tiny step back to raising these children. Let's say we all decide that no matter our race, ethnicity, social class and sexuality, we're going to do e.v.e.r.y.t.h.i.n.g to have our child/ren be happy (sound familiar?). And that, to the best of our abilities, with the resources we have we will do what we can to secure this for them. Your way will be different than mine. We each have access to variables that will affect what we can do, what we see as important, and what we do. Typically, mothers will want to make their children happy. As do many fathers, of course. A no-brainer, *right?!*

Except there are problems with this. Children, rightly so, are assumed to have desires, rights and a voice. Hypervigilance around the *'Are you showing up as a good enough mother?'* blame cycle contributes to an intense need to provide happiness and be responsible for our children's happiness. Conversely, if a child is unhappy, mothers become responsible for reversing that unhappiness. The stakes are high for mothers to deliver and sustain happiness to children and because kids are now, in Jennifer Senior's words, *"economically worthless but emotionally priceless"*, this job is firmly in the hands of mothers. Dedication to this task has become part and parcel of over-intensified mothering; vigilant, attentive, all-in mothering, where 'failure' is not readily tolerated.

In the past ten years, a move towards children expecting and needing their mental state to be a focal point of discussion and attention has been established. Thankfully, this is an improvement on the times when their emotions were brushed aside as unimportant. Once though, the undulations of adolescence were expected, and the isolation of mothering youngsters was not as acute and potentially complex.

Government spending cuts in the UK and Wales youth service amount to a staggering 70% in less than a decade and leave, as Sally Wheale says, *"young people… condemned to become a lonely, lost generation with nowhere to turn"*. Notwithstanding this, they have the support of their mothers, who'll be deemed 'bad' if these young people get into trouble. Youth services historically provided leisure, sporting and enrichment activities often based around youth centres, as well as targeted provision for vulnerable young people, including teenage pregnancy advice, youth justice support, and drug and alcohol misuse services.

It's not mothers' fault that we're one of the only safe havens left for children, but we almost certainly become pathologised in a system that offers paltry regard for our own wellbeing. It's worth mentioning that community mothering models cut across the white-centric mode of individualist parenting. Communal mother-work among those in non-white cultures affords inter-generational support as well as non-biological family input.

To feel responsible wholly for making sure our children are happy is an unattainable goal. It can never be guaranteed. The continuing happiness of our children is not necessarily a result we should even attempt to achieve. This might seem heinous. The emotional landscape of small and older young human beings is not static and holds multiple competing priorities at any one time. Being mindful of getting hooked into their most pressing yearnings, while being there to hold space, can prove a tricky tightrope walk.

For some years now, I've been hearing words along the lines of, "I can only be as happy as my unhappiest child" and "I need my kids to be happy or I can't be happy either" and finally, "my happiness is conditional on my children all being happy". Mothers assume responsibility for the the task of not only instilling but also buoying up happiness. It's key to remember there's a difference between putting in place the best conditions we can for our children to be happy, and being *in charge* of making other people happy.

It is better to teach our children to be in a relationship with their mental health, along the continuum, rather than to educate them that mummy is responsible for making sure they are happy within themselves. This is false Mother-Stopping Noise and it doesn't help them learn emotional regulation, or navigate the world with the inner skills they're going to require.

Most of all, let's return to mothers and the distinction that must be made. To lovingly invest in creating conditions for our children's happiness to be present and flourish is a wholly obvious activity but to give ourselves responsibility for creating, and then maintaining, happiness within our children, is way beyond realistic control.

Mother Stopping Rules, Happiness and You
Celia Dodd pulled a few punches when she critiqued "*if women don't follow the rules, they risk damaging not only their children's health but that of future generations*".

Ouch. When was the last time you let *that* Noise take full shape in your life? I'm willing to bet it's been there for a while for many mums, but it's powerful to see it written so bluntly. We've talked about Noise as narratives, now let's reshape that a little and talk about Noise as rules.

Again, depending on your individual set of circumstances, you may have more rules to bend over backwards for than I do:

1. What Mother Stopper rules are you bending over backwards for?
2. What power structures are they attached to? There might be multiple ones here to consider.
3. How are these rules shaping your ideas of being responsible for your children's happiness?
4. If you don't feel responsible for your children's happiness, what Noise shaped that? (I'm confident there's some Noise in there, even if it's counter to the louder Noise!)

5. Imagine breaking the cardinal rule that you are responsible for your children's happiness. What would this free up in your life? What new (more expansive) rules could you make instead?

*When people say, "at least you've got loadsa kids"
and "best to spare the planet, eh," they blush and
low laugh like we're in on the same dark joke.
Waking in the night, I take out a small box from
under our marital bed, spread the photos, and take
her in, only for a moment; but it's enough. My
husband, asleep, encourages me in the day to move
lightly into the future. No magic spell morphs her
away. I put the broken pieces of myself back clum-
sily, knowing by now my marriage has holes at the
knees. Searching for a patch, I say yes to another
military move. And in the flurry of packing boxes,
school moves, and finding a home, I feel two feelings at the same time.*

Heartbreak and hope.

*Madeline's death teaches me that without heart
we've nothing. This becomes my passion; collect-
ing hearts. Post-it notes, notepads, and jewellery.
I dream of an oversized blank canvas to splash
blood-red paint up and onto. This image haunts*

me as I unpack in our new place. I'm tired of unfurling our hotchpotch home and making it work. I'm tired of sharing a bedroom and crave a space to itch my nipples and sit unwashed.

I line up my dildo collection on a white wooden shelf in the bedroom because they're pretty. And pack them away again when I calculate the date I'll deliver our next baby. Higher than high risk, the following few months are a practice in living with terror. We buy a doppler and become experts at finding the heartbeat. Night and day, I search for the steady beat of life.

Hope and heartbreak, by now loved-up bedfellows.

She arrives at a time when I hate how my husband chews his food. And although I know he needs to breathe, I'd prefer if he did it somewhere else like Sierra Leone, which is where he deploys a couple of years later. Still, I'm in love with my tiny girl. A love that can't be matched right now by a lolloping husband who likes to be praised for doing a.n.y.t.h.i.n.g. The marriage lasts on and I swallow a yes to say 'clever boy' often. After all, I'm used to cheerleading the kids. In a home cram full *of over eighty-seven hearts strewn across walls, in kitchen drawers, on clothes, and everything you can think of that can have hearts on, my own heart stands still.*

I'm a mother of ~~eight~~ seven, consulting in boardrooms, and at the same time, I know to not take any of this for granted. I'm lucky and grateful, but I need more. For me. Just me. Only me.

I begin to talk with my husband about this urge and am met with, "you have your work, you have me, you have the children, what else would you do, Danusia?" In an instant, I taste what it is to be made abnormal. I won't be wronged for wanting to be a full-lusting human being. I'm hungry for myself. All I can come up with in my head is a fuck-me-hard-and-often affair or an expedition to the Antarctic. Hot and cold extremes.

The solution lands in my lap almost as soon as I clock my desires. I'm chosen to be part of a historic polar expedition. The preparation entails dragging a tractor tyre three miles every day for what turns into eighteen months. Through mud, in lanes, buggy out front, tyre attached to my bespoke harness out back. I build up my power in a tightly braided lifeline of facing my fears, holding faith, and I'm so afire, bridging discipline with my dedication to wholehearted living.

As I train I replay my husband's "there's only room for one explorer in this marriage, and it's me" blurt and it anchors me. I am flouting this and rewriting myself by dragging tyres. Not one shred of guilt present. Inadvertently, I make myself terribly ill with overtraining, and this strength making project finally ends the unravelling ball of my marriage. He goes to Africa, where I can no longer hear him breathe or chew.

I stay being an explorer.

THE NOISE SAYS MOTHERS
WILL FEEL GUILTY

We're told to be a mother is to be guilty – isn't that the truth! The notion of maternal guilt is so pervasive in our culture as to be considered a 'natural' component of motherhood. Furthermore, the idea that guilt is a necessary component of mothering is widespread (Seagram and Daniluk, 2002). To read a popular press book or piece of research on motherhood is to read about guilt. That mothers experience guilt in relation to their roles as mothers is the most prevalent finding in mothering research, although it's not been explicitly researched with any depth. It is, as Adrienne Rich said of mothers: *"the guilt, the powerless responsibility for human lives, the judgments and condemnations, the fear of her own power, the guilt, the guilt, the guilt"*.

Mother's guilt, as presented in the media and the everyday lives of women, is inescapable. Popular magazines such as Good

Housekeeping, Psychologies and Diva, offer mothers tips on managing or coping with guilt. The assumption that this guilt exists goes uncontested. From Anna Faris, who said, *"motherhood is like a big sleeping bag of guilt"*, to Erica Jong's quip, *"show me a woman who doesn't feel guilty and I'll show you a man"*, and onto Jane Swigart's words: *"the guilt that many mothers feel is endless and tyrannical. Guilt for providing too much attention or not enough, for giving the child too much freedom, or not enough. The guilt of the working mother, the guilt of the mother who does not have to work, the guilt of the mother who tried to do both – work part-time and mother part-time – and feels both jobs suffer because of it…the guilt of the mother whose child is showing signs of disturbance, unhappiness, physical illness; the certainty you've somehow damaged your child permanently, no matter what you've done or fail to do"*. The core experience many mothers bet on is feeling guilty – it's *assumed* guilt is a universal experience and the inevitability of guilt is accepted.

Guilt, it's said, happens when mothers realise

or suspect transgression from expected behaviours, actions or beliefs. As we know, mothers operate under society's gaze with clear characterisations of 'good' and 'bad' mothers (no s.h.i.t sherlock). In a 2012 study, Miriam Liss, Holly H. Schiffrin and Kathryn M. Rizzo explain self-discrepancy theory, in which guilt is the result of internal warring between *"one's actual and ideal selves"*. Not only this, the fear of negative evaluation and perceptions also contribute to feelings of guilt. In other words, falling short from the 'good' model of motherhood translates into even more layers of guilt.

Feeling guilty is persistently put forward as normal, and the paradox of living a guilt-laden motherhood life is unproblematised, which is surely a problem in itself? Mothers strive for some high standard (unclearly defined AND different according to who you are) OR try to meet expectations set by others. Several factors play into this acceptance of guilt as a normal feature of motherhood; the desire to achieve the perfect model, the expansion of 'expert' advice rendering mothers less trusting of their own intuition, focus on the acquisition of consumer goods, and, of course, social media.

Some mothers live close to family (where support and guidance about mothering might be available), but this is not possible for many mothers, who turn to social media to create support networks instead. Social media has become a vehicle for the construction and reaffirmation of mothering, and a mechanism for supporting mothers in their role (Patricia Drentea & Jennifer Moren Cross, 2011). Mothers' understanding and experiences of motherhood are affected deeply by social media. It's evident mothers interact with and create representations of themselves, other mothers, and motherhood through social media. The very act of reading social media posts is a form of interaction and participation that can affect a mother's thinking, so it isn't only about actively posting within social media forms.

Lack of a face-to-face community means mothers turn to social media to find other mothers who seem like them, can provide validation and who can, perhaps, reduce their feelings of guilt. One Edison Research (2020) study found that 87% of mothers surveyed used some form of social media, with Facebook being accessed most among what they call 'social media mums'. Long-running debates about the quality of mothering in so-called 'Mommy/ Mummy Wars' enacted online accentuate divisions between stay at home mothers and those who work outside the home. In doing so, they (potentially) fuel contributing Noise about what constitutes 'good' mothering. Coverage of this 'war' positions stay at home mothers as closer to the ideal of the intensive (good) mothering model, and the working mother as less involved with her mother role. Simultaneously, stay at home mothers are called, as Jocelyn Crowley puts it, *"inadequate in terms of their being fully functioning adults"*. But let's be cautious because these mummy wars may overstate the prominence of this debate in the real day-to-day interactions between mothers. Although, it's important to mention some mothers do find divisiveness to be present in interactions between mothers.

The sheer force of repetition in mediated messages may create a heightened perception of both this division for mothers and the role of guilt in motherhood. External Noise about intensive 'good and perfect' mothering models is prolific on social network sites, however nuanced they are for Pinterest, Instagram, Snapchat, Linkedin, or Twitter. Each offers the opportunity for mothers to engage with perfect homes, sparkly clean children, hetero-normative ideal relationships, career/baking/fashion/_____(fill in the blank yourself), and arrays of accomplishments, financial success or aspirations you may have. It's likely whatever your internalised version of Noise on mother-hood is, guilt can be triggered from engagement on these social networks. Idealistic mothers, by definition, are of course blissfully happy making themselves available to their family. Or they're platformed as career Super Women and/or positioned as seven-figure entrepreneurs. Naturally, they're not bored, angry or unfulfilled.

Unrealistic Noise about mothers has been influenced by celebrities, Pinterest projects, mummy bloggers, and picture-perfect Instagram influencers for close to a decade now. TikTok, meanwhile, ushered in a different wave of viral motherhood. This isn't the first platform to provide the middle-aged mum community with a fresh, or even silly outlet on the internet, but it's offered an easy way for 'regular' mothers to lip-sync videos, show pranks and create comedy sketches. But TikTok, like any other social network site, is not a utopia and it is not guilt-proofed. Call-outs about toxic mothers-in-law show that guilting other mothers is rife, as one example of how Noise operates. As ever, when the actual experiences of motherhood are seen to be and felt as inconsistent with the' good' model of motherhood, guilt is the product.

As an aside, men tend not to report levels of guilt matching women's (offline and online). This may be due to the meanings women and men ascribe to mother, father and worker, underscored by the fact mothers tend to be 'awarded' unrelenting and total sense of responsibility for the health, welfare and development of their children. Provocative feminist Germaine Greer has a point in these words, *"women feel more guilt than men, not because of some weird chromosomal issue but because they have a history of being blamed for other people's behaviour. You get hit, you must have annoyed someone; you get raped, you must have excited someone; your kid is a junkie, you must have brought him up wrong"*. Greer's brilliance here (heinously lacking though in her approaches to human rights violations, as well as her transphobia in other work) smacks of her trademark challenge to accepted concepts of women's obligations. So, what does guilt lead to?

Mothers second guess how others judge their mothering, and these perceptions give shape to a sense of self as guilty mothers. Lynn O'Connor, Jack Berry, Joseph Weiss, and Paul Gilbert's work reveals significant links between women's mental health issues, such as depression and anxiety, and guilt. Susan Douglas and Meredith Michaels not only describe women as guilt-ridden but also say this guilt co-occurs with and is exacerbated by feelings of inferiority, exhaustion, confusion, fearfulness and anger. Guilt is not necessarily productive, and mothers attempt to participate in what could be described as reparative acts – apologising for their mothering, confessionals about failing to meet expectations, attempts to mend perceived damage and even social withdrawal. Guilt is not homogeneously felt, and it's displayed and acted upon in multiple ways.

This lack of homogenous experience includes several facets, including structural and cultural differences. For instance, money does not guarantee reduced levels of guilt, but knowing one's children are housed, fed and cared for makes a difference. While one mother might feel guilty because her child has not accessed a preferred school choice, another mother may feel guilty because of a lack of resources to clothe and feed her child. The notion of 'good mothering' crosses race, ethnicity, social class and sexuality – ask a mother, and she can almost certainly tell you something about what her culture expects a 'good mother' to look like. For example, a 2004 study of childcare, found *"different social groups navigate differently through alternative 'norma-tives'"* (Duncan et al., 2004), What contributes to guilt for white, middle-class mothers will be different from what racial or ethnic minorities, particularly those with low incomes, experience. Since mothers are positioned as never really living up to expectations of the culture, NO mother can feel confident she is following the 'right' path.

Let's dig deeper because two aspects of maternal guilt are especially insidious and toxic: 1. The Noise says guilty mothers are the most loving mothers. and 2. Guilt is essential to ensure mothers are invested in their child/ren.

This guilt hinders the expression of the divergent needs' mothers might have, vis-a-vis, with their children. Guilt serves as not only a barometer for how much we love our children but is also inextricably linked to the amount mothers are willing (and able) to deny their own needs. It's no surprise to hear that feeling torn between ourselves and our children is required in the current model of exacting moth-erhood. Remember: our truest calling and our

truest place in life are still, regardless of feminist gains, to raise children. Mothers willing to
devote themselves to a place behind their children are deemed the good ones; their needs,
desires and fulfilment must be secondary and
must be compromised. Guilt is another form
of mental and emotional preoccupation with
our children. Put another way; guilt is a powerful cultural tool for manipulating mothers
into excessive investment. Unsurprisingly, this
supports the interests of some individuals more
than others.

Now let's consider mothers who don't experience guilt, though it's a wonder any mother
escapes without the negative self-evaluation that
so often leads to guilt. Are there mothers who
manage to not torture themselves, somehow?
Because, this is a form of self-torture, after all.
What's ironic is that non-guilt-laden mothers
end up feeling guilty for not feeling guilty
because it's assumed we <u>must</u> all be guilty for
something, if not everything. That's not always
the case, as guilt doesn't keep all mothers in
their place. How do I know this for sure? It's

simple; I'm a mother who rarely experiences what I hear many other mothers describe when they speak of their guilt.

One of the opportunities of being the mother of an over-sized family is the way it demands I work out ways to be efficient and productive in the face of a great deal of hard work. Ad-hoc methods would cost me time and that, as we know, is finite. I figured out, within a couple of my first children before I was twenty, that guilt takes inordinate amounts of both time and energy. If I worked on the assumption that I had a load of time to waste, then I allowed guilt to seep into my marrow. Once inside me, this guilt gnawed away, and the more I heard others talk about their incapacitating levels of guilt, the more I wanted to grip it. This was the first stirrings of my unpacking the central tenets I'm speaking of here in this book.

IF, as research suggests, guilt acts as a constant indicator of a mother's love and a stabilising and regulating mechanism, I had to ask myself, privately, some hard questions.

Did guilt ensure higher levels of my love

for my children? And if not, did guilt, at the very least, mean I'd provide better stable care for these same children? In my case, I was clear that guilt did not operate in those ways, at that time. Conversely, I found once I got clear on who I wanted to become, rather than what I wanted, my perspective on guilt changed. This is nothing to do with money, status, happiness or anything situational. In some ways, it was pragmatic, based on practical considerations, like I can't be in two places at once so I'd better get very clear and at peace with my choices. I didn't involve myself in the game of guilt, which is, after all, mere Noise.

Sidenote: When I was working and I missed my baby, I used this to consider adjustments and if these could be made (sometimes they were impossible). I committed to not turning this inward on myself since this cost me the precious gift of time and drained me of my energy, which in turn affected my mental health. Guilt-less mothering became an intentional practice of mine, and still is to this day.

Beyond my example, there are plenty of what

Andrea O'Reilly calls, "*performances of outlaw mothering*", in which mothers intentionally engage in efforts to challenge the power and dominance of intensive mothering. In most cases, these 'bad mums' (also known on social media as naughty mums, slummy mums, or slacker mums), aren't bad mothers at all. Of course, they're not. They're fed up with the message that mothers are under pressure to do it (the home, mothering, relationship, career) perfectly, all the time. These (mostly white) mothers' rebel against and reject idealistic (and utopian) versions of motherhood presented on mainstream and social media. Often, these are as unrealistic and performative as the intensive mothering Noise they critique, but they allow mothers to engage with conflicting identities as mothers and women. Ultimately, mothers respond in some way to the Noise about guilt. As Audre Lorde pioneered on this, "*I have no creative use for guilt, yours or my own. Guilt is only another way of avoiding informed action, of buying time out of the pressing need to make clear choices*".

Guilt, Guilt and More Damn Guilt

Adrienne Rich sure said it when she refer-
enced the "fear of her own power" in relation
to mothers and our guilt (or lack of). Mother
Stoppers are wildly volatile on the notion of
guilt and the teeny tiniest possibility that we
as mothers hold the key to our children's ruin
feeds the guilt and keeps it fat.

Let's starve it a little:

1. What guilt shows up in your version of
   motherhood – and, is it good or bad?
2. How are your versions of Noise shaping
   the ways you feel guilty?
3. If you don't feel guilty, what power
   structures or belief systems are aiding
   that? How is not feeling guilty shaping
   other Noise in your life?
4. Erica Jong said "*show me a woman who
   doesn't feel guilty and I'll show you a man*"
   – What Mother Stopper cultures exist to
   reinforce maternal guilt in your life?
5. In what ways are you keeping your guilt
   fat? What would happen if you stopped?

Motherhood's toll feels personal; it's like the illusion of armour, except it's paper-thin. I 'yes' my dreams while inhaling stories of women combining kids with giant purpose, as many as I can muster in sittings that last years. Sometimes tragic, I skip the part where they kill themselves, intentionally or by calamity. Lingering less on tales of women giving up on themselves, I dissect forensically for clues; which conditions nourish mothers to create beyond kids?

I'm seeking patterns, and the aha's of these foremothers. I want to know what's at the heart of how they build undiluted selves while doing all the work bringing up children takes. In a misstep, I suck myself back into rescue fantasies of handholding, happy-ever-after, toast crumbs in bed. This is easier than facing myself head-on as single. Oscillating between business, brunch dates, and cocktail bars, I ~~interview~~ meet prospective partners in a carousel of lewd to sinister moments. Nestled in the middle are men with ordinary bad breath, great on paper attributes, and suspect grammar. Occasional miss-starts help me create a practice of performing candlelit eulogies for: 1. Men who disappear despite declaring love, 2. Men desperate to move in after the first date, and 3. Keen lovely men, ill-equipped for the remit. Girlfriends adopt eulogy cleansing too and it becomes a reverential local habit of profound power.

It's a summer, or four, of adventures. I still search for a recipe to rise higher. The more I sink myself into finding purpose and contribution to the world beyond kids and a future spouse, the more all's good. The minute I hook myself onto any kind of sacrificial model of being a mother and woman, the less things are happy, for us all. It feels obvious and, at times, risky. Yet I can't do it any other way.

I seem to need to reconfirm my complete love for my children, at least to others, as I explore who I can be. It's not that I'm doing anything wild or weird, but the audacity of not fitting neat categories (married, employed, tethered, tamed) is noteworthy. Scrutiny comes with daring to unpack *what it means to be a woman devoted to herself as much as to her kids. It's suspicious. Although, that might be more the red satin-lined leather mini skirt I wear to ride my beloved bike along the beachside. I say no to the question of whether I'm a high-class hooker – the imagination in this tiny seaside town is running on low. The idea that I live without a husband, laugh a lot, and gad-about doing something internationally, <u>must</u> equate to sex work. It's a classic two add two to get seven.*

Setting aside my shock (and seething), I see how dangerous a woman alone and in charge of herself must be. So. Very. Unsettling. In a match-burning-in-a-crocus moment, as if right on time, I am met. The tall, handsome deep voiced Doctor soothes locals whose lungs exhale the panic of one less woman on the loose among 'em. It's an instant click, blending as easily as any mid-life professionals can with exes, broods of kids and hundreds of miles between us. We shatter being single for an Us. My job of finding self-determination isn't going away just because we're joining the dots of our lives.

Atrophying any part of myself, or sublimating for the sake of a whole, just isn't on the cards. I'm fighting for myself all the way through the difficult days he brings, and as (messy, acrimonious, old) layers surface from his past. I mustn't lose my urgency to go beyond keeping my head above water (kids, career, his career, his kids, obligations) and I'm watching I don't fucking fall apart at the seams. Whispering to myself, 'you have this', I calculate the price of paying my own way, not just in money, but in holding tight to a sense of myself that's unoccupied by others. I'm getting a mouthfeel of gravel, unkinking all the zigzagging of creating a togetherness. My step-kids are holding onto dislike to dislodge me, while my own adjust to a different thrum.

The wording must fit here – nothing fancy-schmancy. In a layered, glorious collaborative process (brief note: old style) I'm pregnant with what we call 'the last baby' – new layer of complexity to unfolding events. I wrap my head around the fact I don't know what's going to happen next.

On the radio in the scan room, Eagles front-man Don Henley sings, "sometimes you get the best light from a burning bridge" as the sonographer announces it's triplets. Then she bursts into tears; it's her last ever scan of a twenty-five-year career, and she's never found the alive beating hearts of all three triplets. She runs from the room, shout-crying the news.

I'm alone with the three foetuses. Mute.

THE NOISE SAYS MOTHERS
AMBITION SHRINKS

Before we move onto this particular Noise, let's take a quick look at a pretty standard definition of ambition: "*a strong wish to be successful, powerful, rich, etc.*" or "*a strong wish to achieve something*" (Cambridge Dictionary, 2020). Given this, it's not hard to understand why ambition is a particular issue for women. The achievement of success, power or riches are not (necessarily) <u>easy</u> for women to attain in many parts of the world. Despite opportunities opening for women, generation upon generation of passed down inner inhibitions still have a stronghold on modern women. As Adrienne Harris explains, "*the psychic price that gender inscription attaches to ambition and strivings and achievement*" is present for many women. Harris highlights key factors affecting female ambition: 1. Negotiation of issues around separation and harmonious relations, 2. Anxieties about aggression, and 3. The unconscious dynamics of an all-powerful maternal idealisation that (potentially) crushes daughter's desires and ambitions.

Women's ambition is a site of much conversation and research. As Frances Arnold mentions, "*personal meanings of ambition vary enormously, perhaps more so for women now than in any previous generation, particularly given that many experience more possibility and choice than previously imaginable*". Arnold gets specific on this when she continues, "*possibility is inaccessible to some American women and to many women around the globe*".

Ambition is especially conflicted and unreachable for women, but not in monolithic ways and not necessarily with the same focal points of 'success'. Before we get into that, here's a definition that offers something different. Dorothy Holmes describes ambition as *"the loving, passionate pursuit of what you most fervently want to become, with perseverance and focus, despite the odds"*. What this definition points to is the crucial need to actualise ambition through a sense of agency. Thwarted and unresolved ambitions are at the root of (some) psychological angst, anxiety and depression. It may be objectionable to make this sweeping statement since white middle-class mothers of means are most likely to consider our-selves agents of our own lives, a privilege other mothers may not be able to access.

Back to those focal points I raised earlier. When ambition is written about, it's often in relation to women and work or motherhood and work, as if these are legitimate arenas for ambition to be discussed within. Arguably, the ambitions of mothers must be tethered to productive outputs, such as a career or creative pursuits, and preferably ones that accrue finan-cial reward. The idea that mother's ambitions develop in a desire to be more of themselves (not for others or to accumulate money) is absurd, not to mention utterly self-absorbed. Which is not something that women, especially mothers, are allowed to be. Development of the self needs to be in relation to others because this will serve the central figures in a mother's life (her children, her husband/partner) better.

Stephanie Brody says that, *"it is not safe for women to forcefully desire self-valuing goals, money, status, or authority. Men, but also women, criticize and demonize women. Those women who forge unapologetic pathways to success, desire to reach higher, or to change social or economic position or policy, can be labeled as disobedient, or unfeminine. When women spill out of the predictable prescriptions of patriarchy, they are regarded as domineering, dangerous, and suspicious. Cast as a dangerous enchantress, "dirty goddess" or a "carnal scapegoat" (Dorothy Dinnerstein, 1999), women who refuse to be seduced, stalked, possessed, and controlled, become targeted, labeled, and indicted"*.

Strong words, but possessing ambition is like walking yet another tightrope. Stephanie Brody talks about this as the thin line between what is expected, what is feared, and what matters most. Being a central figure in one's own life, is not what is expected once women become mothers. Critical to the subject of ambition, Adrienne Harris cautions us to answer not only the question, *"what does a woman want?"* but importantly, "*what woman, where, and in what historical epoch?*".

It could be said that contemporary white middle-class mothers are used to being treated and treating themselves as autonomous individuals, which motherhood potentially undermines. Self-efficacy, a crucial deep belief in the power to deal with the challenges and failures that arise along the path towards actualising ambitions, will hopefully be present. This self-efficacy is built on beliefs about the ability to influence events that affect our lives. Which is all well and good, but each mother is "grounded" within a larger social context (Lynne Layton, 2004) which means ambition will be limited, facilitated, and deeply affected by the world into which each is born. As Stephanie Brody says, "*culture, racism, social class, gender bias, and misogyny bring layers of impact, an encumbrance that burdens healthy development. Can we ever know when our desires have not been altered by influence, when our "choices" have not been pre-determined?*"

Let's take a commonplace example. Women's

ambition and the shrinkage of it when women become mothers has been proposed over and over. On top of this, there's the stubborn theory that women are less ambitious than men, inherently. Add in their children and the Noise goes that their ambition plummets. Whether women's career goals change with the arrival of children or not, the link between reducing levels of ambition and maternity itself is **not** proven. If anything, research demonstrates that ambition doesn't diminish. Women start careers with just as much ambition as men. A study of more than 200,000 respondents found that women's ambition levels do vary, but this is unrelated to motherhood and instead linked to company culture (Boston Consulting Group, 2017). Ambition is not a fixed attribute – it is nurtured (or damaged) by the daily interactions, conversations, and opportunities that women face over time within organisational cultures.

Research conducted by Jean-Anne Sutherland showed racial variations in labour force participation regarding feelings about working outside the home. Many respondents in her study discussed negative evaluations of themselves, which was widespread amongst both white and Black mothers. Similarities ended there, as white mothers spoke of the need to work outside the home to manage and/or avoid becoming "baby brained". These white mothers justified working outside the home to "become better mothers". Being more present for their children was achieved because of their careers. Conversely, Black mothers relished the chance to be there for their children because this has not typically always been an option.

As Kimberly Seals Allers points out: "*Historically, we have always worked and mothered. Many have even grown up seeing their mother and grandmother work more than one job. This is all we know. So, the notion of having time to mother feels unfamiliar. There is still the social stigma of taking time off to mother – something black and brown women have never felt free to do. Ever since our bodies and our babies lost economic value, we have struggled to reassert our value as mothers and our importance in raising our own children. As I often say, black women in this country are viewed as perfectly acceptable and desirable for taking care of other people's children but somehow stereotyped as not being able to take care of their own".*

Hence, the can-you-have-it-all debate is not only ridiculous but blindingly white-centric. To peddle the misperception that a woman's ambition takes her away from her rightful place at home tending to her children and spouse, and that the career is secondary to domestic gender roles is to speak only to some mothers. As Dionne Powell argues, *"there continues to be an uneven playing field that is more uneven the further you are from white male hetero-normative archetypes".*

Despite this, there's evidence that Black women may be "more ambitious" than white women, but struggle with disturbing invisibility around securing significant leadership positions (Melinda Marshall and Tai Wingfield, 2016). Leaning in (with ambition), as Sheryl Sandberg famously wrote about, is not the same for everyone – something she forgot to mention. Voluminous research and attention are given to women's problems, including mothers rising to leadership roles within the workplace. As Eve Rodsky starkly puts it, *"the strongest bias against women, is motherhood"*.

A growing body of research shows mothers pay a significant wage penalty for having children (Michelle Budig and Melissa Hodges, 2010), while 40% of employers say they would avoid hiring a woman of childbearing age (Slater and Gordon, 2014). One in nine mothers felt forced to leave their jobs, and 77% of working mothers reported a negative or possibly discriminatory experience during pregnancy, maternity leave, or on their return from maternity leave (EHRC 2016). Other areas of concern include the struggle to balance their careers and mothering roles (Sandra Faulkner, 2012), experiences of working in contemporary organisations (Patricia Lewis, 2014; Minna Nikunen, 2014), and maternal employment (Eric Holmes, Jenet Erickson, & E Jeffrey Hill, 2012). Another concern is not only negotiating breastfeeding in the workplace (Noortje van Amsterdam, 2015), but enacting it, which means mothers "*navigate the separation of the traditionally feminine, private realm of reproduction and the traditionally masculine, public realm of production*" (Paaige Turner and Kristen Norwood, 2014).

And then there's the crushing issue of childcare. Childcare expenses consume pay, and some mothers decide to leave the workforce as a result. Typically, mothers are the ones who make this trade-off. Expanding mothers' access to affordable child care and other workplace support is vital, as families are increasingly relying on mothers' incomes.

One study found that, between the ages of 35 and 50, the clear majority of educated women working in white-collar professions (a whopping 91% of American women, 81% of British women, and 89% of German women) say they're driven to succeed. Of this same group, (59% in the US, 72% in the UK, and 66% in Germany) women earned at least as much as their spouses (Sylvia Ann Hewlett and Melinda Marshall, 2015). Approximately 42% of mothers are the sole or primary breadwinners in their homes

(NWLC, 2017). Black and Latina mothers work at even higher rates. They are more likely than white women to be the primary bread-winner in their households, with 71% of Black mothers and 41% of Latina mothers serving as the primary economic support for their families (Sarah Jane Glynn, 2017). At the same time, women are disproportionately working in low-wage jobs with nonstandard hours and inconsistent schedules. Many of these mothers struggle to find affordable childcare that aligns with their work schedules and available during evenings and weekends. Childcare challenges, coupled with low-wages and irregular sched-ules, make it difficult for many mothers to stay in the workforce – whether full or part-time.

Mothers are differentially positioned in social statuses that can, and do, affect employ-ment outcomes. In amongst this, white women have used the labour of women of colour to reduce their/our own domestic burden and free them/ourselves up for corporate and civic pursuits. Those who are married and have access to a husband's income may face different incentives for working and career advancement than mothers who are unmarried or who have low-earning husbands. White women have different opportunity structures than non-white women that affect decisions about education and employment; in turn, these influence life-course trajectories of work advancement and earnings attainment.

It's unsurprising that mothers take their ambitions out of corporate arenas if they enter them in the first place. Leaning out, AKA trading in corporate jobs for entrepreneurship, is common. Mothers who leave the corporate world in droves often state they left to focus on children, when they are really railing against structural conditions so hideous, the choice might as well be viewed as being made for them. One study scratched beneath the surface for the reasons why women leave the workplace. It uncovered that women **aren't** leaving to look after children, which this study found was simply a "socially acceptable answer". The study found many women went to another job or started their own company, asserting that, *"we need a perfect storm of flexibility, pay, communication, so that women want to stay in the workplace"* (Kristin Haffert, 2019). Excessively long hours that preclude involvement with their children (mothers being seen as ideal caregivers whether this is the case or not) become proof of dedication to a job that means mothers must keep two feet in a career at the same time as two feet in the home. Essentially, two full-time roles – it's no wonder mothers can feel torn between the systemic oppositions of profit-making and people-making: work and family.

'Good' mother ideology stands in direct opposition to that of working mothers. The dominant idea on repeat by nearly every cultural entity – government, media, corporations, our friends, our families – is that being a mother with ambitions and raising children are irreconcilable pursuits.

Mainstream discussion about mother's ambition seems too often to land at the level of mindset. Much anecdotal social media coverage of 'success' as a mother is about either adopting morning practices and/or flipping belief patterns that allow mothers to learn 'how to shine'. But this can't be all about women's mindsets and belief patterns; it's inextricably linked to structural inequalities. We know that even as workplaces are changing in terms of the presence and space for (some) women, reproductive and domestic work (the care of the family) has changed much less.

Wanting a self, one that's centred in our own life, is a revolutionary imagining. A life with self in the centre rather than at the edges. Women's ambitions, and especially mother's ambitions, become shrouded, derailed and clouded by the centred needs of our family first. Then there's work which acts as another legitimate repository for some mother's ambitions, with all the time spent grappling with working within corporate landscapes that benefit (many) men and a few women.

As the painful realities of divisions and privileges surface, the words of Audre Lorde come to mind, "*the quality of light by which we scrutinise our lives has direct bearing upon the product which we live, and upon the changes which we hope to*

*bring about through those lives. It is within this
light that we form those ideas by which we pursue
our magic and make it realised".*

———————————

A Mother's Ambition

I can't honestly decide where the Mother Stoppers
are loudest: on our guilt or our ambition. Maybe
it's a combination of the two – with all the Noise
making us feel guilty about being ambitious.

Similar to the ways mothers are 'allowed' to
practice self-care, there are often <u>very</u> defined
ways that mothers are 'allowed' to be ambitious:

1. What does the Noise say your ambition
   is 'allowed' to look like in your version of
   motherhood?
2. How is ambition connected to the ways
   of being a good/perfect mother for you?
3. How has the Noise and/or Mother
   Stopper culture tied ambition to being
   a good/bad mother in your version of
   motherhood?

4. In what ways is ambition tied to your children? Consider emotionally, mentally, financially and creatively. For example, are you responsible for all childcare costs – how does this impact your financial ambition in terms of earning potential?
5. What power structures or culture divides hinder your ideas of ambition for yourself as a mother?

If there's a moment for me to surrender, it's during this triplet pregnancy. Growing three babies is a monumental ask. Imagine everything in triplicate; the sickness, tiredness, and anxiety. It's impossible to avoid medic-risk chats; selective reduction, screenings, and mortality. Being sensible includes not getting my hopes up while hoping for the very best outcome. It's a heartfuck. Everything changes from scan-to-scan as the babies grow, stop growing, and restart. Watching their progress as Baby A, Baby B and Baby C is a torture. A bittersweet waiting for the axes to fall. It's hard to stay up when it's unlikely to pan out well. Connecting with a tiny army of Facebook women in the same position is a lifeline. Some cradle triplets, many don't.

I'm working in boardrooms and advising in heels, interspersed with puking in executive loos. It'd be funny if the stakes weren't so high. Given I birth early with one, it's a battle to get much past viability. Every day counts. One day in the womb is worth four days in an incubator, I hear at the hospital. I am told to do my best with as little stress as possible. Side Note: the day I asked my red wine guzzling fiancé to get help for his reckless habit, or go, he shoved a few belongings into two Tesco bags, and left. It's guts that'll see this through, and I sit with this aftermath of grief. What a cockwomble.

Am I deliriously scared? Shit-bat uncertain? Every single day. BUT SO WHAT! Nobody puts these Babies in a corner.

Alright, real talk: it's my job to get these babies born. It's all that's required of me and I'm doing this anyway. There's no in-between. I'm relying on myself – no matter what happens.

*And guess what? **I motherfucking did it!** Eleven born, ten living: Freddie, George, Jack, Tom, Harriet, Isadora, ((Madeline)), Meredith, Montgomery, Seraphina, and Horatio.*

Fast forward two years, and I'm raising triplet toddlers, teens, and supporting older ones in all sorts of ways. It's an almighty hokey-cokey; they move out, they come home temporarily, and so it goes. I've learned to juggle breastfeeding triplets, despite having two breasts, found an office the size of a broom cupboard minutes from our rented home to (lie down in) work from, and managed to get through countless surgeries with the three little ones. Being so premature they need 'repairs'. At which point, perimenopause showed up.

Which is when I sat down and wrote to my kids. It'd been brewing for a while. There wasn't any significant event that prompted it. Nothing that meant I had to write, it was simply time to say these words.

Here's the short letter I wrote, and emailed, to my children, unprompted and with a certainty that this _had_ to be said:

To my sons and daughters,

I'm writing this because I want to share with you an important piece of information that sits at the heart of our relationship. It powers who I am, the kind of mother you experience and fuels my desire for you to be an independent, happy person when you're grown up. I could wrap this up for you in layers of niceties, yet it's best to straight shoot it: you're not the centre of my life. Shall I repeat this in case you didn't catch the sentiment? You are not the centre of my life. I wouldn't blame you *for wondering if I'm in a mood or something but please know I feel as far away from crazy as you'll ever find me. Because the message I'm sharing, changes everything, and nothing – you're not the centre of my life, <u>AND</u> at the same time, I love you more dearly than words can possibly express.*

I'm sharing this now because it seems to me there's a persistent story peddled, about you being more important to me than I am to myself. I'm sure you've come across this or will do – but I think this idea is the thing of madness. The proposition that I make you the centre of my life rather than myself as the core player feels both ludicrous and downright misleading.

How can I, for instance, teach you what it takes to be a fully-functioning emotionally-intelligent independent life-skilled human being when I'm living my own life dependent upon you (my children) as my source of fulfilment? That doesn't make sense to me. But it really does seem to be what's demanded of me, and what you're being told to expect.

You'll probably find right through your childhood there are mothers who put themselves last (or somewhere low down) in their own lives. It's probably because they've been taught that to be a good mother, they've to consider everyone else's needs before their own. They'll be the mothers that forget who they are because they shelve themselves over and over daily, weekly then yearly. I guarantee you'll see mothers who think it's their job to sacrifice and compromise themselves as a mark of devotion to their children.

These mothers might also be the livid ones, the ones who seethe under fixed smiles and the ones with exacting requirements for their kid's successes. After all their children's successes are a direct measure of their own worth hence their children *must* do well – it'd be hard to watch a child's life unfold in ways that don't match a set picture if you've given yourself up in order to raise that very child!

Instead, my love for you doesn't depend upon you being an extension of my unfulfilled dreams. My love for you is borne of an excitement to see the person you become in your own right and in ways you choose, irrespective of me. I'm able to wholeheartedly relish your independence in part because I've not cut my own potential off or small-sized myself because of you or your siblings. There are bound to be times when we disagree about things along the way (right?!), but, as co-travellers on life-affirming paths I love myself and you completely. And that makes a difference.

Your Mum

THE NOISE SAYS MOTHERS
MUST BE SEXLESS & SEXY

When I was an academic, I published not only about leadership theories and cross-cultural methodology but also on hedonistic consumption. How this latter area of research came about gave me an insight into the 'meat' of the Noise surrounding mothers and our sexuality.

In a business school meeting, to carve out who was supervising which thesis, we allocated proposals to each academic according to expertise and interest. For the most part, this was an easy task, although sometimes a line of research would 'snafu' the process. This was the case on the day in question. My male colleagues and I had been working diligently and eventually arrived at a proposal with a focus on the Pink Pound. This is often called Pink Money because it describes the purchasing power of the LGBT+ community, which has gone from being a marginalised market to a thriving global industry. In 2019, LGBT+ adults globally held a combined buying power of approximately \$3.7 trillion (Nick Wolny, 2019).

Instead of our typical, efficient conversation and allocation, there was a hush. The Chair of the meeting took the proposal and, in one precise glide, pushed it down the table to me. The rationale he gave was that, as a woman, I seemed to be the best supervisor for this particular student's work; I'd have to get myself up-to-date on all things Pink Pound. Everyone else agreed, and the Chair moved onto the next student.

On meeting my supervisee, I confessed I knew nothing about the Pink Pound, but I was fully invested in learning about it. He suggested I immerse myself in this learning – and that's how I ended up accompanying my postgraduate student to an Erotica Expo in London for the weekend. It was an education. There were things I couldn't unsee. In a stroke of fortune, I discovered an area of research no-one (at. all. anywhere.) had researched previously. Because my male colleagues assigned the sexually-focused Pink Pound project to me, I found an entirely new research territory; sex shops.

For more than three years, I researched and published on the inside world of sex shops, with a special interest in women-only retail contexts. The publication I especially loved writing is called *'It's Business Doing Pleasure with You'* – and not just because of the witty title. My Pink Pound student unintentionally opened up this research avenue that positively impacted my academic career because this area of hedonistic consumption (as it's called) had never been penetrated.

It's interesting to note what research gets done, and what remains taboo. The 'why' of the silence on my new research area was obvious; who wants to spend months hanging around and working in sex shops? No male academic, that's for sure. And it seems that's somewhat similar for research about motherhood, sex and sexuality. Scholarly interest in mothers' sexuality appears both low and paltry.

The first barrier to conducting any systematic research on mothers and sex is the fact that motherhood sexuality is a taboo. Mother, sex and sexuality are words rarely seen strung together (Holly Zwalf, 2020) for one ultra good reason; mothers aren't supposed to be sexual, or at least, *some* mothers aren't. In her book *Of Women Born* (1976), Adrienne Rich pointed out that mothers' experiences of sexuality are not just personal but institutional – constructed and regulated by a patriarchal society. So, what is it about motherhood and sex that's so incompatible?

Let's look at the contradictory mechanisms at play here. Famously, Caitlin Moran asked: *"Do you have a vagina? And do you want to be in charge of it? If you said yes to both, then congratulations! You're a feminist"*. Congratulations aside (given many modern women are cautious about labelling themselves as feminist), being sexually in charge of ourselves is of interest to me. Is it that mothers' expressions of sexual agency are intimidating and of threat somehow? If we rewind historically and include religion, especially Christianity, we see it's commonly blamed for shaping moral systems that perpetuate a madonna-whore dichotomy in Western culture. The madonna is pure (even virginal), holds high morals, is gentle and supportive; whereas the whore is seductive, promiscuous and dangerous. An extreme spectrum of sexuality becomes apparent. This creates conflict for women since the integration of the sexual self, and the maternal self isn't smoothly reconciled; sexuality and motherhood become mutually exclusive. This navigation and integration of mother self and erotic self translate into an impossibility that Vivienne Cass calls, *"measuring up to the ideal of the Madonna while also being comfortable with themselves as sexual beings"*.

This split sets up an asexual-sexual dichotomy (also called the madonna-whore archetype) that divides mothers into 'good' and 'bad'. The good mother is wholly fulfilled by her children (focused on their needs and the epitome of the good and perfect mother model) while the bad one is anything but. The 'bad' mother might fantasise about finding her own G-spot as she stirs baked beans for her kids at tea-time, God forbid. *Kimberly Ann Johnson* puts this well when she tells us: *"For centuries, cultures have placed sexuality and motherhood in opposition. A woman could not be both a mother and be sexual. We are still struggling with this inheritance".*

Numerous long-standing myths about sexuality and motherhood have yet to die away, including, 1. Once a woman has children, she is first and foremost an example and must be conservative in culturally specific ways. (If we need a surprising instance of socially constrained maternal sexuality, we need only look at Deborah Sundahl's seminal book on female ejaculation, *Female Ejaculation & The G Spot* (2003), with the tagline '*not your mother's orgasm book!*' on the front cover. Supposedly, 'your mother' and mine wouldn't need this book which is damning and, at best, confusing). 2. Sex is for procreation, and 3. Mothers are presumed to have sex with their permanent, male partner because 'healthy sex' is defined by research, educational and medical professionals as vaginal-penile intercourse. This is seen as 'real sex' which excludes women for whom this is not their preferred sexual activity. Research on maternal sexuality is based on heteronormative sexual acts, highlighting a serious flaw and deficiency.

Many new mothers experience ambivalence about the transformation from sexual to maternal being. Not surprising, given all the Noise upholding the asexual-sexual divide. As a reminder, ambivalence means having mutually conflicting emotions; however, our linear society misunderstands that holding two or more seemingly disparate feelings at the same time is wholly possible. This holding of two positions at once mirrors expectations of maternal sexuality, as Audre Lord tells us: *"On the one hand, the superficially erotic has been encouraged as a sign of female inferiority; on the other hand, women have been made to suffer and to feel both contemptible and suspect by virtue of its existence. It is a short step from there to the false belief that only by the suppression of the erotic within our lives and consciousness can women truly be strong. But that strength is illusory, for it is fashioned within the context of male models of power".*

Many mothers will testify that the desire for a fulfilling sex life doesn't disappear when we have children; it simply gets buried under an avalanche of conflicting demands on our time and attention. Becoming a mother does change our relationship to ourselves sexually (for some, it's transitory, for others temporary, and others still, long-lasting). Nevertheless, this change is not a given. Exhaustion, along with postpartum physical changes (sore vulval area, c-section recovery, engorged breasts progressing to cracked nipples, hormones spiking etc.) signal a refocus from sexual intimacy to maternal intimacy. Mothers are sexual beings, but Audre Lorde is right when she told us, *"the erotic... has been made into the confused, the trivial, the psychotic, the plasticised sensation"*.

Sexualised Noise for mothers, whether about sexy maternity bras, pregnancy photoshoots (a legacy triggered by the infamous Demi Moore cover shoot in 1991) or ping-back-after-birth pressure does not disrupt the idea that asexuality goes hand-in-hand with martyrdom. To give up one's sexual agency in favour of one's children is, at the very least, the legitimate and acceptable face of motherhood. Although, let's be clear, what's being discussed here is white-middle-class hetero-motherhood. Cultural norms of the asexual mother are intertwined with a celebration of white femininity and heterosexuality that don't apply to all mothers. To be asexual is to set aside needs and desires of your own, or at minimum to put needs and desires on hold OR be perceived as a bad mother. This elevated form of motherhood – selfless and sacrificial – is, as we know, at the heart of so-called 'good motherhood'. Since freedom and independence are cornerstones of desire, women who attempt to be 'good' mothers forgo these and relinquish this aspect of themselves. Asexual mothers (or ones who hide their desirous sexuality) are seen as caring and dedicated to their family. Doting mothers just don't have lusty sex.

Or do they?

IF we consider sex as including play and pleasure, it's hardly a leap to locate why mothers are disallowed desire, arousal, and adventuresome light-my-(own)-fire turn-ons. Good mothers are supposed to be turned on (in this case, let's say lit-up) by their children. Sexual agency isn't the end game for good mothers. As Holly Zwalf says, *"poor, indigenous and Black mothers have been, and remain, fetishised and hypersexualised, portrayed as irresponsibly promiscuous and seductive as opposed to the modest chaste Western white mother"*.

Robyn Longhurst expands on bad/deficient mothers when she writes: *"Lesbian mothers are thought to be lacking a man. Mothers on welfare are thought to be lacking financial resources. Drug dependent mothers are thought to be lacking will-power and the self-control to quit their drug habit. Mothers who do not live in nuclear families are thought to be lacking in "proper" families. Teenage mothers are thought to be lacking in maturity and mothering skills"*.

The list of bad mothers is potentially endless, and the regulatory Noise loud.

Before we explore 'bad mothers' further, let's remember that motherhood and sexuality research typically represents only the pregnancy and postpartum periods. Vivienne Cass describes four phases of motherhood during which mothers may experience sexual difficulties or experiences – briefly, these are 1. Trying to get pregnant, 2. During pregnancy, 3. Postpartum phase of six months following birth, and 4. Living with a baby, then toddler, then a small child. It's surprising that she, herself, truncates the description of mothers sexuality at the point when mothers are raising small children. However, navigating maternal sexuality intensifies when our children become strapping teenagers who, themselves, are exploring their emerging sexual selves. This presence of teenage children who stay up late and are close to bedroom areas where a mother may (or may not) wish to be sexual can bring issues.

Picture the scene. Let's say I bought a vibrator. First, it has to make it past young questioning eyes and eager hands who open post as soon as it arrives or request to open any package. Then, once in my bedroom, this vibrator will need to be stored in a place where teens (who go through every item as if it were their own) cannot find it. Next, there's the noise of this vibrator, possibly and probably heard through the walls or down the hall. Literal Mother Stopper Noise, if ever there was!

Teenagers investigate and interrogate mothers about new objects, noise and 'what she's up to'. In part, this is because mothers' lives are not viewed as our own. This includes our sexual selves, albeit many children, including adult children, will hope their mother is not sexually active or avoid thinking that this is even possible. Yes, Mother Stopper Noise reverberates across generations.

Let's return to mothers who the Noise says occupy the sexual/whore end of that dichotomy (it's depressing even to write that sentence, but it needs to be done). Mothers situated outside the heteronormative-model of motherhood are seen as unacceptable and unworthy. Julie Thompson, the author of *Mommy Queerest (2002), advises: "While lesbians are excluded from legitimate maternity because of their ostensibly reprehensible erotic desires and practices, heterosexual mothers are excluded from the enactment of a non-procreative sexuality lest such activity be construed as immoral"*. A queering of the maternal opposes heteronormative motherhood and means lesbian mothers are *"constructed as bad mothers because, like gay men, they are associated in the popular imaginary, with sexual activity"*, which conflicts with the madonna ideal reserved for white married heterosexual mothers of means.

Let's also look at how Latina mothers are portrayed in the media because this depends significantly on age. The hypersexualisation of Latinas from teenage years through to their forties is well documented across media settings. Older Latinas (in films) are single mothers, wearing tight clothes, continually going on dates, and casually sleeping with men. Here's the plot change though, these same mothers always become devout and chaste once they become grandmothers. These stereotypes place Latinas on an extreme spectrum where suddenly, with age, mothers shift from being seen as sexual all the time to having no sexual urges at all. These stereotypes, especially when they work together, are harmful because they limit the scope of Latina sexuality (Loubriel,

2015). Additionally, this false representation also places age limits on what it means to be sexual and reinforces a racialised madonna/whore dichotomy.

Lisa Rosenthal and Marci Lobel researched racial stereotypes within motherhood and compared Black and white mothers' perceived sexuality. Black mothers were perceived as more likely to be sexually promiscuous, engaging in more unprotected sexual activity, and having lower socioeconomic status, than their white counterparts. Conducted in the United States, this study found Black American women also continued to be stereotyped as poor, uneducated, young, single mothers who sleep with and use men for money ('gold diggers'). They're stereotyped as purposefully having children to take advantage of public assistance programmes and unable to provide financial resources to adequately care for their children (Roberts, 2002). The authors' findings support their hypotheses that there are negative stereotypes about Black women related to sexuality, motherhood, and socioeconomic status, consistent with historical images of the 'Jezebel' and 'Welfare Queen' archetypes.

The study also provided evidence that when healthcare professionals, consciously or unconsciously, hold negative stereotypes, their attitudes can lead to discrimination in the provision of care and health outcomes for mothers, contributing to health disparities (Shavers et al., 2012). Stereotypical images *"resulted from and justified the oppression of Black women in slavery, including the sexualised abuse and exploitation of Black women to the benefit of white male slave owners"* (Sublette and Sublette, 2015). These continue to affect people's perceptions and judgements about Black mothers. Evidence has grown that Black women's experiences with discrimination (grounded in intersecting Noise about Black women's sexuality and motherhood), both throughout their lifetime and during pregnancy, predict a greater risk of adverse birth outcomes. These are not petty differences between the way white mothers and Black mothers' sexuality, motherhood and healthcare are viewed and subsequently treated.

In the UK, a national population-based study found that 56% of pregnant women admitted to hospital with COVID-19 in pregnancy were from Black or other ethnic minority groups (Parliament UK, 2020). Operational policies and tailored communications need to reduce stereotypes and responses to Black women and other ethnic minority groups, in more socially just ways.

And then there's the vitriol launched at heterosexual mothers who try to occupy excess sexuality alongside motherhood. Ashley Wright, who went viral for practising pole dancing while breastfeeding, shares, *"the experience of being able to do an act and live a life that demonstrates strength, balance, sensuality, nurturing, motherhood, power, grace, divine femininity, and then some, all at once, is freeing"*. As she explained to Caroline Bologna, *"it's my #blackgirlmagic"*. To go public as a pole dancing, breastfeeding mother rendered Wright an unfit mother; the combination of maternity with 'excess' sexuality is not tolerated or tolerable. In this case, what's important to mention is how

Wright's body was already hypersexualised as a Black woman. Natasha Pinterics sharpens our understanding when she says, *"the dual positions of Black woman and pole dancer create a firestorm of reactions about the threat of the excessive, sexual maternal body"*.

The Noise tells us (some) mothers are deemed asexual and sexual simultaneously. Let's take the acronym MILF which refers to 'Mother-I'd-Like-to-Fuck', a term coined in internet newsgroups during the 1990s with the earliest reference a 1995 post about attractive mothers. The term MILF was popular in the 1999 film, *American Pie*. In light of the general erasure of maternal desire from both feminist and popular texts, MILF might seem to be an improvement. As May Friedman argues, *"this fetish/genre of sexual expression at least acknowledges that mothers do, indeed, have sex. Mothers who are presented as femmes fatales are at least immune from the sanitised and insipid assumptions about mothers as exclusively caregivers with no erotic engagement"*.

Yet MILF is a minefield of contradictions of

what Nina Martin calls a *"tyranny of sexiness"* since mothers are positioned as objects via a male gaze, rather than sexual subjects engaging with maternal desire. May Friedman suggests that Nina Martin's tyranny of sexiness reminds us that *"mothers must selflessly live for their children while remaining well presented, busty, and red-hot after the babies go to sleep"*. After all, MILF's are expected to be insatiable in the bedroom but selfless mothers outside of it.

What isn't openly discussed is the proliferation of the MILF genre of porn (including popular pregnancy and lactation sub-genres). This archetype takes away maternal agency and maternal desire; rather than being about mothers who like to fuck, mothers get fucked, in every sense of the word (Friedman, 2014). While the MILF archetype would finally seem to enable the possibility for sexualised motherhood, it presents this hope only as a passive undertaking. Mothers anointed with the title MILF don't own their sexuality; they're owned.

Set beyond a pornographic context, the socially acceptable, appropriate packaging of maternal sexuality in the MILF archetype could show progress in that it marries sexuality and motherhood. It has the potential to resist and shut down sexual shame. But, and it's a big but, it's also essential to remain mindful that an embrace of fierce sexuality and motherhood is not a safe choice for everyone (Friedman, 2014). Silence and shame are the major contributing factors to the irreconcilability of sexuality and motherhood. For instance, punishing mothers in custody disputes is a common weapon; hence a contradictory asexual-sexual (sexless-sexy) dance/ is attempted.

As an important aside, mother's eroticism is channelled (albeit differently and of course, non-sexually) into their children. For many heterosexual mothers, their focus doesn't revolve around their male spouse any longer. Instead, their children's development, their playdates, and their overall needs come first. As Esther Perel shares, *"female eroticism is diffuse, not localised in the genitals but distributed throughout the body, mind, and senses. It is tactile and auditory, linked to smell, skin, and contact; arousal is often more subjective than physical, and desire arises on a lattice of emotion".*

The physical relationship between mothers and children constitutes a host of visceral experiences – hugs, rocking, cradling, kisses, gentle pats and strokes, smiles, winks, laughter, eye contact – and for many women, by the end of the day they have 'nothing left to give'. Intensive mothering, with that one woman round-the-clock mothering machine as the principal protagonist, alters the focus of many mothers who, in an attempt to infuse romance into relationships, schedule 'date nights' akin to the ways playdates are managed. Esther Perel argues this full-contact parenting competes directly with intimate adult relationships. Gender notwithstanding, whoever takes the children's primary caregiving role tends to follow a pattern; loss of self, a tough job disentangling from household chores and responsibilities, plus submersion in all things to do with the children. This is a stark reminder of my house husband experience shared earlier! In case you're wondering, this isn't specific to heterosexual couples either (Perel, 2007).

On the physical connection between mothers and their children, let's explore breastfeeding and sexuality. Some heterosexual mothers choose not to breastfeed because it makes their male partner jealous. Iris Young suggests that *"if motherhood is sexual, the mother and child can be a circuit of pleasure for the mother, then the man may lose her allegiance and attachment"*. This might sound an exaggeration – the jealousy of a man whose own child gleans nourishment from the mother's breasts – but overall negativity about breastfeeding may support this proposition. The Noise about public breastfeeding highlights discomfort about the breast as a sexual object, especially when it can be both publicly seen, and at the same time draw attention to suckling as potentially pleasurable. It isn't that all mothers find breastfeeding a pleasure (they don't) more that public breastfeeding is transgressive. It has been traditionally repressed, hidden and denied; a mirror for mothers' sexuality. As Holly Zwalf says, breastfeeding as *"site of pleasure and not one simply for service"* blows open the sexless selfless mother ideal, again.

While we focus again on the Noise about allegedly sexless/asexual mothers, it's clear; historically, disability has been shown in limited ways. Portrayals of what disabled studies scholars recognise and critique as 'Super Crips' (individuals who've overcome a disability) or those portrayed as objects of pity are the most common stereotypes. But disability is not a monolith. In her book *Sitting Pretty: The View from My Ordinary Resilient Disabled Body (2020)*, Rebekah Taussig writes of conflicting emotions surrounding a memory of being catcalled. As a woman, she's horrified; but as a disabled woman and part of a community historically thought of as childlike and asexual, she finds herself revelling at the moment. She explores how disability has largely been left out from discussions of feminism and many feminist debates (on the wage gap, reproductive rights, and the problem with seeing 'women' as a homogenous group). I'd add mothers, sex and sexuality are not anywhere near complete without discussing the intersection of disability.

The barriers to sexuality facing mothers with

disabilities include the stereotype that disabled mothers are not sexual. Assumptions about sexuality, motherhood and disability almost certainly lead to this lack of research interest with disabled mothers. The general invisibility of disabled women in our culture (except for individual heartwarming stories of overcoming adversity) contribute to this exclusion. As Kristi Ketz says there's also that *"unimaginable idea of disabled women being mothers since that notion confronts our stereotypical notions of motherhood, and/or the inconceivable thought of disabled women as sexual beings"*. Contrary to pervasive societal stereotypes, disabled mothers have fulfilling sexual lives (Judith Rogers, 2006).

Whether denied sexuality or over-sexualised, mothers are constrained by notions of **appropriate** maternal (sexual) behaviour. As we navigate a hypersexualised and sexist society as mothers, we can examine how our Noisy world could be different. Reassessing the quality of all aspects of our lives – including sexuality – is a must. Part of this is {re}claiming our right to *"an assertion of our life force"* as Audre Lorde called it in her essay *'The Use of the Erotic: The Erotic as Power'*. Or as J. J. Halberstam encourages, *"we must be willing to turn away from the comfort zone of polite exchange… in order to fail, to make a mess, to fuckshit up, to be loud, to bash back, to speak up and out, to disrupt, assassinate, shock, and annihilate"*.

You Sexy Mother (?)

Sexuality for women has long been a minefield, ready to blow up in our faces with one wrong footing. That minefield becomes entwined with increasingly complex acrobatic gymnastics to avoid explosions once we become mothers.

The Noise is shrill on the morality of how mothers should (and should not) present or openly explore their changing desires, intimate and sexual, once they have children. But it's an incredibly vital area – vital *need* – that must be embraced.

Taking your unique version of motherhood into account, let's explore how this is showing up:

1. In what ways has your sexuality changed or been shaped by motherhood – what Noise is this connected to, if any?

2. How are ideas of being a 'good' mother connected to your intimacy and sexuality – for better or worse?

3. How does the Noise support you celebrating your sexuality as a mother?

4. How does the Noise prevent you from exploring your sexuality as a mother?

5. What repercussions do you imagine from the Noise or Mother Stoppers for embracing your sexual desires as a mother?

6. What would (re)claiming (if you need to, you may have already) your sexuality as a mother mean for your sense of fulfilment in life?

When I was seventeen and in labour, a midwife removed my glasses, while another muttered under her breath, "just in case". I didn't know why she'd taken them without my consent; I understood later. Without my specs, I couldn't make out anything other than my own little hand in front of my face. I began to feel helpless, just as a consultant anaesthetist entered the room and announced I was being prepped for a non-elective epidural. He instructed me to get in the correct position for the procedure, then barked I looked barely twelve and ought to be in a schoolroom, not about to give birth.

The combination of his contempt, coupled with my inability to see what was being 'done to me', left a stark imprint. I vowed no-one would ever again remove my glasses. Over the years men tried, especially those wanting to prove I'd be "so much prettier without the goggs". But I never forgot what it felt like to be in the dark and exposed. I rarely revisit the ugly hell I swallowed down.

Lockdown changed (all) that.

Whatever I write about this almost-a-year can't span it; from global dissolution and change to an entire upending of life as before.

Feeling in the dark and exposed means I search for ways to keep us from being bitch slapped by Covid. Because I'm an 'us', right?!

*Bubble sealed. Masks on. Risk slashed, **maybe**. And I'm back in that room, near-blind and clueless.*

Doomscrolling gives me the runs. Rock-and-a-hard-place.

Old style memory-making disappears. Goodbye to outings and our well worn <u>tiny</u> bunch of happy activities my disabled one can face. Gallivanting with him is a no anyway, as he can't walk far unless he can. It's complicated. Now, even those choices evaporate.

*#StayingInMyLane is the ONLY way forward. The **less** Noise, the better.*

In vulnerable times, the mundane remains. The steady hum of things that must be done. The ordinary. Food. Laundry. Bills. Beds. Obligations that build stability but get a reputation as miserable.

This isn't about entertainment. It's an exercise in stamina. Repetition is Queen.

Because whatever's been lurking in the shadows, emerges in lockdown, surely?

It's a long time since I drank alcohol and I stay without it. Distracting myself with anything but chunks of dark salt chocolate just doesn't happen. Besides a night in bed with Tony Goldwyn, in a vivid dream that lasts. I crave more than snatched calls with friends but, work + kids. Voice notes are a lifeline.

Lying in the dark and exposed, the words "all the women. in me. are tired" backs me into a sob.

Thank you for that, Nayyirah.

*The **less** Noise, the better.*

I begin documenting numbers; of laundry baskets, homeschooling lessons, meals cooked, picked up dog poo, orgasms, fights I've broken up between the kids, and more. It's a fucking mish-mash of life.

Except numbers can't capture the grief, the losses, the cumulative impact of this pandemic. It's individual, nuanced and still here.

The small things matter.

Burned banana bread wolfed down in minutes. Cuddles on the sofa with nowhere to go. Sub-zero alone time yet a growing love of tiny cabins and a chainsaw called Ruth, after iconic RBG herself. Who incidentally shared, in order to make things work in a marriage and at work, it sometimes helps to be a little deaf.

The less Noise. The better.

THE FUTURE: NOISE & MOTHERHOOD

This book is written and set within exceptional and unprecedented times, globally. Most research on motherhood and parental penalties/premiums in the workforce examine these areas during stable, or at least, non-pandemic economic conditions. The effects of parental status in shaping employment outcomes during periods of economic crises, such as those created by the COVID-19 pandemic, are much less studied. There are several reasons why, during economic downturns, employers may rely on gender-based stereotypes as they are forced to respond to precarious conditions. Laying off workers, reducing hours and reducing wages are typical strategies, but cultural beliefs of mothers as expressive caretakers and fathers as active breadwinners (deserving of career advancement) help shape employers' decisions. One concern is that COVID-19 is exacerbating existing patterns of parental status and gender inequality in organisations. Results (so far) suggest this worry is valid.

One study in late 2020 reported how employers were less likely to lay off fathers following the outbreak. In fact, fathers were less likely to be laid off compared to mothers and non-parents. As Felipe A.Dias, Joseph Chance, and Arianna Buchanan found, *"mothers are 66 % more likely than fathers to be laid off in the outbreak period. We also found that the "fatherhood premium" was higher among lower-educated and mid-educated workers, which is consistent with prior studies that show that the motherhood penalty in earnings is largest among lower-skilled and mid-skilled workers".*

Women are almost twice as likely to be employed in sectors classified as essential. Ethnic minorities of Indian, Pakistani, Bangladeshi, and East-Asian descent are also disproportionately more likely to be employed in sectors not included in the UK lockdown from March 2019 onwards. By implication, these workers were (and still are) exposed to work in which there's a high risk of contracting the coronavirus (Lucinda Platt and Ross Warwick, 2020). Equally, mothers, particularly lone mothers, were more likely to work for shut down sectors. Almost 40% of working single mothers with the lowest level of qualifications were employed in lockdown sectors prior to the crisis (Richard Blundell et al., 2020). Those employed in occupations for which working from home was possible are least likely to have experienced financial hardship during the first phase of lockdown, but as the pandemic continues the total effect intensifies.

Structurally disadvantaged groups – women, racial-ethnic minorities, and working-class – are more exposed to long-term unemployment and poverty. This is all within the context of already high barriers to employment, formed during a pre-existing recession. What is known is that *"approximately 35% of all workers faced a substantive loss of income – i.e. "COVID-19-induced economic hardship" – between March and May of 2020"* in the UK (Richard Blundell et al., 2020).

The enormity of caring for and educating

children at home differentially impacts families. Those who are better off, with higher levels of education, and the space to do so, are better able to juggle work and education activities simultaneously. Plus, they may also have savings to cover unforeseen expenses. Poorer families, especially single mothers, have been adversely impacted by crippling pressures from childcare and work. We must remember that almost 40% of working single mothers, with the lowest level of qualifications within this group, were employed in lockdown sectors prior to the coronavirus crisis (Richard Blundell et al., 2020). This picture is stark. The uneven responsibility between single mothers and non-resident fathers is one under-examined type of injustice resulting from patriarchal social arrangements.

This pandemic has forced a smidge of a way toward recognising collective responsibilities and dependencies; that we're *all of us one accident or illness away from needing others*" including state benefits (Independent, 2018). Turning to married/partnered counterparts in a report by Lean In and McKinsey & Company

(2020), more than 70% of fathers reported they split household labour equally with their partner during Covid-19 lockdowns. But only 44% of mothers say the same. In a School for Mothers Report (2020) for the UK Government Women's and Equality Committee, only 3% of mothers mentioned supportive partners. On the back of this Sheryl Sandberg discusses the plight of mothers as not just doing double shifts anymore but a *"double-double shift"*.

The potential for a change in social norms because of this pandemic, is evident. An increase in remote working could be beneficial for mothers' careers. However, if it's seen to benefit only mothers, how will this touch mothers' status quo of being primary/best caregivers with subsidiary roles as workers? It could be the longer hours fathers are spending with their children during this pandemic accelerate some changes, but so far there's not been documented evidence of reduced inequality in childcare time between men and women. An even balance in childcare might happen over time, but it's too soon to see if this is borne out. As much as the COVID-19 crisis brings a chance to make our family lives, domestic arena and workplaces fairer to mothers, it's clear multiple systems of oppression decrease the likelihood of this happening. It's an opportunity, but one that will take systemic unpacking of privilege to shape our society for the better.

This is a time in our cultural history when we can use our power to influence and create profound change. We can seize this moment as an opportunity, although at times it seems a losing battle, to grapple this culture and its Mother Stopping hatred of mothers. We must fight to cut through all this Noise and create new conditions. Being a mother and mothering is a powerful social change modality, not to be taken lightly. We **can** achieve social change through mothering (tenderly and mindfully, with respect for the systems of oppression that affect us differently). Parents of any gender can have social change impact, but it'll be mothers who will be the leaders to shape our narrative, rather than having others shape it for us because any story's power lies in the hands of the storyteller.

Joan Peters once said, *"we must face the uncomfortable fact that most women do not live up to their potential because they have succumbed to the maternal ideal. That is, they do not continue in their true character – ambitions included – once they have children because they are afraid to demand accommodation from their male partners and society. This is an issue of identity and – of the soul".*

Almost twenty-five years on from Joan Peter's words and we know life and mothering are vastly changed – yet this over-masculinised world continues to dominate the Noise of motherhood.

The Opportunity We Now Face

I want to bring us back to the idea of these central pillars I'm talking about being Noise. The way I've framed this may make it sound as though we can remove or 'end' this noise, once and for all, but that's not the case. Neither should we want it to be. The Noise will shift and change, but it will always be there, in some form.

Noise can be helpful. It can point us in the direction of change and connect us with others. We all add to the Noise, in different ways, so perhaps what is more important for us to think about is how we would like the noise to sound in our individual life, and how we're going to contribute to it in **valuable** ways:

- ✧ *Which pieces of motherhood Noise work for you?*
- ✧ *Which pieces could you (if you want to) redesign?*
- ✧ *Which Noise is entwined with your social locations?*
- ✧ *Which Noise endangers you, and your children?*
- ✧ *Which Noise is a priority for you to change?*
- ✧ *Which motherhood Noise do you not want your children to inherit?*
- ✧ *When will we feel safe enough to cast aside the good mother model entirely and rewrite our own versions?*

If we don't begin to reframe it in this way,

if we don't reorchestrate the Mother Stopper Noise, we'll fail to be the architects of our own motherhood. Ultimately, we're responsible for how we rebuild this framework.

And we don't have to do it alone. I believe **Mothers are agents for Social Change.**

Individually and collectively we have everything we need to untangle ourselves from the conditioning of the Mother Stopper Noise. As Malkia A. Cyril said, *"mothers are a key vehicle for social change."* Our collective expectations and how we continue to exert them needs to be re-examined. We internalise what we are fed within our cultures and continue to feed ourselves with it. In return, WE dish this out to other women and serve it up to our children (remember: Contributing Noise). Our daughters, and just as crucially our sons, learn what to listen to by the expectations we allow into our households.

We can't expect our children to grow up thinking mothers have value, unless we actively occupy that value ourselves. If we don't, if we lose ourselves, we teach the people we love, whom we've created, that mothers are only a conduit for their success and happiness. We teach them that mothers exist solely to shepherd other people's lives to fruition, but not their own. Or that mothers may only do it around the edges of other people's lives, picking up the crumbs of who they are when they can. That mothers come last, if at all, in comparison to the lives of everyone else around them.

As mothers, we navigate reclaiming ourselves against a cultural tide of self-negation. No-one wants to liberate mothers and it is NOT because WE are individual failures; it's because systemic barriers exist that stop us. These systems have been built in ways that thwart us, it's why we get tired not only with the exquisite privilege that is mothering, with its relentless repetition, domestic constancy and enduring resilience that's the epicentre of raising functional, happy children, but because we're battling against systems that simultaneously invite our talent to be productive in the economy but tie our ankles together (metaphorically). We're left without a chance of moving in directions that seem, let alone are, self-serving, agency infused, and self-fulfilling. Our free labour as mothers is the glue holding society together. No one wants to fully answer the question of what would happen if mothers were allowed to choose themselves because that would be the grand undoing of everything we've come to know in our society.

In this book, I've presented you with the six core pillars that have stood firmly in my life, as a mother, that I've had to actively choose to take a sledgehammer to. Refusing to be a prisoner for a version of motherhood that *I* decided doesn't belong to *me*. It is not an easy thing to do amongst all the Mother Stoppers and their Noise. It's why I've included questions along the way because adhering to this Noise without question means we become complicit in our own oppression. Eve Rodsky started this idea in her bestselling book *Fair Play*, where she put forth the acronym CIYOO – Complicit In Your Own Oppression. Every time we make excuses for our husbands or spouses, our children, our bosses; we are complicit. Every time we acknowledge that something doesn't serve us but continue to engage with it, we are complicit. We take it on. Jane Hardwicke Collings hit it home for me when she said, "*on my deathbed, I really, really want to know that I have done everything I could to make sure that the things that I think really matter are secured for the generations to come*".

We MUST create a new legacy for our children, or this NOISE will continue.

What a terrible burden for our daughters to bear; to know if they choose to become mothers, this will be their fate too. Because if we show them that being a martyr is the highest form of love, that *is* what they will become. They will believe they have permission to live only as fully as their mothers allowed themselves to live. Glennon Doyle frames it well when she says, "*if we keep passing down the legacy of martyrdom to our daughters, with whom does it end? Which woman ever gets to live? And when does the death sentence begin? At the wedding altar?*

In the delivery room? Whose delivery room – our children's or our own? When we call martyrdom love we teach our children that when love begins, life ends. This is why Jung suggested: There is no greater burden on a child than the unlived life of a parent".

Why is the 'good and perfect' mother ideology crap persisting? It begins with how we mother our children. The gender definitions we create in our homes, expand outwards into our communities, who feed it back to us, and round and round we go. We need decent caregivers; invested, emotionally literate, present caregivers, and we need to start valuing caregiving. We need to strip the idea of caregiving as being a 'female' role and make more room for men to enter that space. I don't believe they don't want to, but the historical gender definitions we keep subscribing to form a locked door for many men. Which is why we need to stop mothering men – they can't become caregivers if we keep mothering them. And we don't have to guess a way forward here, there's enough good theory to help us.

Kyl Myers describes the success of raising her child on gender-neutral terms in her book *Our Adventures in Gender Creative Parenting* (2019), advising, "*instead of us telling the children who they should be, maybe it's the children who will teach us how to be. We just have to get out of their way*".

We are teaching our children these central pillars of motherhood are the way forward and they're not. We must teach our daughters not to continue this, whatever *this* is. And in this book, it's not just daughters – we must teach our sons what's needed too.

How do we imagine that our children are going to inhabit a different kind of world if we do not give them a context within which to have that world? We say we want it – that different world -, but we don't know how to get it. So, we get little chunks of it, but we need to <u>do</u> something different.

I don't have all the answers. I do have the conviction that we – mothers, fathers, parents, *all* of us – can be the agents of social change our children need. That we *can* throw out these systemic, toxic belief systems about motherhood. I *have* to believe that and I *have* to keep working at making it the only truth. For my own children and for myself.

This is my manifesto. I hope it helps you find more of yours too.

From the Heart

I first set out to write a book that answered all the questions I get asked. The ones about having so many kids yet still being dedicated to my own growth, success and work. A fellow triplet mother, friend and author, Stephanie M., mentioned me to her publisher, who then asked me to submit a proposal. Writing this book wasn't something I chased, even though I'd been asked several times before to write my secrets, nudged to share my formulas, and flat-out poked to get my story down so others could learn from it. I knew this would be of interest to others because every time I come away from giving a keynote on stages, there's a let-down moment when I tell people *"no, I've not written a book telling you how to make it all work*". There's an old maxim that says we must listen to what people ask us for as it's what the world wants from us. So, thank you, first of all, to the crowds of women (and men) who called on me again and again to write about motherhood. I'd written about this as an academic, but not since. You all knew best.

Back to that book opportunity; I wrote flat out for seventeen hours straight to produce a meaty proposal for the book I thought I would write. It was a step-by-step practical, how-to, advice guide, with a flavour of polemic. Submitting it to the publisher reminded me of being an academic; publishing was part and parcel of my career portfolio. Frankly, I had to grow large ovaries to get over the worries about potential rejection(s) in that phase of my life. The commissioning editor, Claire P., said it was an impressive proposal. When the senior editorial team discussed it, they agreed but hated the original book title and were dismayed at my cut-throat commercial bio. But they did like the overall pitch. Signs there would be a book deal were there.

As much as I felt this first iteration would be interesting, I had this weird sense it was an empty set of manoeuvres, plastering over deep cracks. Sure, I could write that how-to motherhood book, but something tugged at my intuition enough for me to resist the momentum. A second publisher and commissioning editor, Nikki M., stepped into the ring and still, I couldn't deliver. Thank you to both cheerleading, publishing-powerhouse editors for your recognition.

The more I sat on this book, the more there was something not-quite-gestated, which was bloody frustrating. I'd clarify the practical systems, the processes, the organisational and systemic barriers and so on, but it still wasn't quite right. I was unsettled and bloody-minded enough to know that forcing anything doesn't *ever* help. I let the book sit dormant. Occasionally, I'd spend a few days on the proposal or chapters, but I was messing about, simply 'playing' at writing. People asked me how it was going and I'd say it was coming along, which saved face. Actually, it was hibernating. Waiting for the right conditions within me, so it could break above ground.

I booked a session with a healer, Sophie B., hoping she'd unlock the door to a tsunami of fast-fire writing. I dreamt of this flow and the subsequent joy that concluding my book would bring. The truth was, I wasn't engaging with the content. I was only focused on the result. Sophie told me something important in our one-time session: *"Avoid reading anything by anyone else. You've got this book within you right now, right here"*. This advice sounds obvious, except it's not. Often writers, especially those with academic backgrounds, rely so much on getting close to other people's work (their arguments, opinions, propositions, and findings) it becomes hard to find our own voice. This healer was telling me to undilute myself and to do it unapologetically.

Like any pregnancy, of sorts, there are dangers in birthing too early. I vowed not to plunder motherhood books for leads. Instead, I plunged deeper into myself. As much as I'd have liked to throw aside this project, it was literally the Noise that would not, and could not, be quelled. Every time I tried to make what I wanted to write the bullseye, I was met with my own internalised Noise about what I ought to be writing. Because let's be honest, there are well-worn (safe, learned, acceptable) pathways to success. However, I realised my job is not to be popular; it's to say what needs to be said.

Which is to acknowledge that being in conversation with hundreds of women collectively, and individually, on a week-in-week-out basis, as host of the School for Mothers Podcast, humbled me. I'm forever grateful to every guest on my show. Their willingness to be open and share their large selves galvanised me and, in the end, I ditched preoccupations with myself. I rallied to the messages that had to be written by me, and only me. After all, I'm not only living my intersecting relationships with Mother Stopping Noise, but also my solutions to these daily. I don't get to operate outside of these constructs any more than anyone.

Which takes me to the moment in time when

I could f.i.n.a.l.l.y bring myself and writing this book together.

In many ways it's laughable that my phase of readiness happened precisely at a time of no schooling, no prospect of childcare, and a home even more full of my children than usual, because older kids too. The time when everything didn't stand-still. The time that lasted and is still lasting, a year on, when mothers, me included, are holding 'the babies, the bath, and the bathwater'. Holding all that weight, and then some. More specifically, the reality of being the carer of disabled children, keeping a business afloat (clients, a remote team), podcast hosting to the tune of ten episodes a month and the juncture of many agendas, moods, and disappointments.

My older ones grappled with, and are dealing with, thwarted home moves, stopped driving lessons and tests, stymied dating, sexual freedom compromised, as well as furloughing, re-engagement with work, and the oddness of finding themselves back at home living a different rhythm and literal life. Then there's covid, which arrived for a grown son who lives away from home. The worry for him and his partner was acute. Meanwhile, my younger ones access school work with differing levels of support (from myself and older siblings) always framed by the oscillating work pressures on us. It's crazy making stuff; decision fatigue is without frills. For me, there was the irony of attempting to write, in and amongst the swirl of all this global turmoil, as well as domestic saturation and all the other parts of myself.

But the writer in me urged me to get this beast of a book out of my system, since it's been growing in significance for years. The certainty that I couldn't tolerate the Noise any longer and stay silent helped. If you will imagine the stomach churn of impending vomit – when the moment is right, there's no stopping the splurge of whatever must come out. As much as this picture is almost violent (when does anyone upchuck gracefully?!) the (p)urge to write this book had to happen. In a pandemic surrounded by children, fueled by these endless noisy questions: How at peace am I with being imperfect, as a mother, as a human being? How tender will I be with my shortcomings? How far will I let go of maintaining an image of myself, for myself, and this image for others? How do I forge my own path within my family and do justice, enough? Because these questions can't be disentangled from the very core of this book; they're at the heart of it all.

Indeed, Madeline, my child-born-still taught me to not only examine the heart in my life, but our fleeting time together was a remembrance to not sleepwalk through it either. I'm incredibly full of gratitude to all my children. It's said that we birth the children we need, and if this is true, it would appear my needs were abundant. Without my darling children, none of this would have come to me, and I'm beyond thankful to be their Mumma. But most of all I'm proud of the generous, much-loved, thoughtful people they have become and are still growing into – as people in their own right. Thanks, kids for being incredible supporters of who I am beyond being your mother.

I'm extraordinarily privileged to work

alongside my eldest daughter each day in the family consulting firm, as well as in everything else. Suffice to say, without Harriet, the gateway to my own mother-wound healing could never have happened. I owe her giant thanks as we move forward into more.

At Triumph Press, I'm indebted to Editor in Chief, Elaine Mead, for her editorial acumen throughout and for being such an astute wordsmith in this process. What a ride!

There are far more people than I can ever list by name here, including circles of Sisterhood that enabled me to keep going on this creative journey. You truly know who you are. Meanwhile, Dickie Van der Sausage, our family mini-Dachshund, injected enormous fun into the times he insisted on being my writing companion. I'm hoping he'll stay steadfast as I complete my upcoming memoir, and this book's companion – SPUNK: a Manifesto Modernising Fatherhood.

And finally, I'd like to thank my mothers, J and P, for being themselves. You taught me, and continue to land, elements of this book that I'm grateful for. Adoption is complex, yet visiting the orphanage room in which I was born, meeting the social worker that took me from my biological mother's arms and handed me to my adopted mother was pivotal. Subsequently meeting you, my biological mum, was a coming home. To witness mannerisms, the face that mirrors mine and to sense millefeuille-like layers of buried loss, was life transforming. I thank you for allowing yourself the freedom of not taking me forward as you built another life. And for striving for the agency to do this. Ultimately, I could not have been the woman I am without my adopted mother. She taught me the inside-out of tenacity, how to whip down curtains and run up a dress with a trusty sewing machine, and the real cost of setting self aside.

RESOURCES

This book is a long-overdue part of a bigger conversation I've been bringing together for a few years across different online and offline communities. These communities are filled with empowered and vital voices, from women, men *and* children, on how we can create the types of mother-(and parent)-hood that allow us to pursue our authentic selves – on **our** terms.

The conversation doesn't stop with this book, and I'd love for you to join me in keeping it going. Here are a few ways you can do that:

⬦ **School for Mothers Podcast** –
Created to stretch traditional narratives around working motherhood and bring ambitious, talented, and diverse,

sometimes underrepresented female voices to the forefront of this narrative, the School for Mothers podcast upends outdated perspectives and interrupts the Noise that surrounds women on how they should 'be' once they become mothers. Launched in 2018, there are hundreds of recorded episodes, reaching a global audience in 97+ countries, and over one million downloads to date. You can find the podcast on all podcast streaming services and on www.schoolformothers.com/podcast

⬩ **School for Fathers Podcast** –
Launched in 2019, the School for Fathers podcast explores modern working fatherhood (not a phrase we hear too often), seeks to understand modern fathering and the challenges fathers face as they reposition their role in work, the family and in society. You can find those episodes on all podcast streaming services and over on www.schoolforfathers.com

⬩ **School for Mothers Online Community** – This group is exclusively for mothers at any stage of the motherhood journey. We don't focus on parenting advice because SFM is all about **you**. This is a welcoming space where mothers share support as we amplify our desires for ourselves while raising the kids we love. This is our sanctuary for mothers who want to access free resources while learning valuable skills. We'd love you to join us: www.facebook.com/groups/schoolformothersgroup

✧ **More Time to Do What You Want: A Game Changing Mini-Course** –
You've things you want to do but <u>everything</u> keeps getting in your way. You're ready for more time and especially more 'you-time' – this mini course is all about the super simple method I created to give me guilt-free time to do the things I want to focus on, for myself. I'm thrilled to share it with you so that you can do the same: www.schoolformothers.com/moretime

✧ **Get Your House in Order: 1 Mini-course & 3 Scripts to take you from 'Doing-it-All' to 'Sharing-it-All'** –

When did 'having-it-all' become 'doing-it-all'? Does your day feel consumed with never-ending housework? Are you tired of nagging to get things done only to end up doing it yourself? If you're feeling at a crossroads and needing to have the conversations that move you and your family forward this is the resource for you. You can download the mini-course, which includes tweakable conversational scripts, to start having the conversations you want to have but aren't, here: www.schoolformothers. com/getyourhouseinorder

A Tiny Favour

I hope that reading this book has not just given you lots to think about, but it's helping you explore how to move forward, for yourself and collectively as mothers together.

As I've said, this book is part of a bigger conversation that we're all a part of. And to do that, people need to read this book (*bit of a no brainer, huh?!*)

Public reviews are a fantastic way to be a part of the conversation, and they're vital for independent publishers in getting the word out and growing the audience of a book. So, a tiny favour, if you do have the bandwidth to share a review and your thoughts I would love if you could do so here: www.triumphpress.co/noise_reviews

BIBLIOGRAPHY

Introduction

Collins English Dictionary. (2020). Glasgow: HarperCollins Publishers.

Crenshaw, K. (1989). *Demarginalising the Intersection of Race and Sex: A Black Feminist Critique of Antidiscrimination Doctrine, Feminist Theory and Antiracist Politics.* University of Chicago Legal Forum: Vol. 1989, Article 8.

Darwin, Z. & Greenfield, M. (2019). *Mothers and Others: The Invisibility of LGBTQ People in Reproductive and Infant Psychology.* Journal of Reproductive and Infant Psychology: Vol. 37(4).

Dow, M. D. (2015). *Negotiating "The Welfare Queen" and "The Strong Black Woman":*

African American Middle-Class Mothers' Work and Family Perspectives. The Work of Motherhood: Vol. 58, pp. 38–55.

Elkin, L. (2018). 'Why All the Books About Motherhood?' *The Paris Review.* [Online article].

Elliot, G. (2019). 'Why Do I Have to Choose Between Being a Writer and Being a Mother?'. *Electric Literature.* [Online article].

Green, F. J. (2012). *Practicing Feminist Mothering.* United States: Arbeiter Ring Publishing.

Gumbs, A. P., Martens, C., & Williams, M. (2016). *Revolutionary Mothering: Love on the Front Lines.* United States: PM Press.

Marshall, J. (1984). *Women Managers: Travellers in a Male Word.* United States: Wiley.

Marshall, J. & Gearty, M. (2020). *Living Life as Inquiry – a Systemic Practice for Change Agents.* Systemic Practice and Action Research. [Online article]

MBRACCE-UK, (2019) 'Maternal, Newborn

and Infant Clinical Outcome Review Programme, "Saving Lives, Improving Mothers' Care Lessons learned to inform maternity care from the UK and Ireland Confidential Enquiries into Maternal Deaths and Morbidity 2015–17'. *Nuffield Department of Population Health*.

Morrison, T. (1981). 'Writing Is Third Career For Morrison'. *The Cincinnati Enquirer,* Cincinnati, Ohio.

Rodsky, E. (Lawyer, Author). (February 2021). *School for Mothers Podcast*.

Rukeyser, M. (1968). 'Käthe Kollwitz' from *The Collected Poems of Muriel Rukeyser*. United States: University of Pittsburgh Press.

Unravelling the NOISE and MOTHER STOPPER Culture

Athan, A. (2016). 'How Academia Studies Mothers'. *Every Mother Counts*. [Online article].

Collins English Dictionary. (2020). Glasgow: HarperCollins Publishers.

Harrison, L. & Rowley, S. B. (2011). *Babies by the bundle: Gender, Backlash, and the Quiverfull Movement*. Feminist Formations: Vol. 23(1), pp. 47–69.

Jordan, A. (2016). *Conceptualizing Backlash: (UK) Men's Rights Groups, Anti-Feminism, and Post-Feminism*. Canadian Journal of Women and the Law: Volume 28, pp. 18–24.

Perell, D. (10, May, 2020). @david_perell on *Twitter*.

Rapp Black, E. (2019). 'Redefining Resilience'. *UNUM Magazine*. [Online article].

Seals Allers, K. (2018). 'Rethinking Work-Life Balance for Women of Color'. *SLATE*. [Online article].

THE NOISE SAYS MOTHERHOOD IS OUR CALLING

Davis, A. (1981). "*Racism, Birth Control and Reproductive Rights,*" in Women, Race, & Class. New York: Random House.

Erdoğan, R. T. (2016). International Women's Day speech (2016) as cited from

France-Presse, A. (2016). 'Recep Tayyip Erdoğan: 'A woman is above all else a mother''. *The Guardian*. [Online article].

Furedi, F. (2010). *Paranoid Parenting: Why Ignoring the Experts May Be Best for Your Child. London.* United Kingdom: Bloomsbury Publishing.

Grue, L. & Lærum, K. T. (2002). *'Doing Motherhood': Some Experiences of Mothers with Physical Disabilities.* Disability & Society: Vol.17(6), pp. 671–683.

Havrilevsky, H. (2014). 'Our Mommy Problem'. *The New York Times*. [Online article].

Hays, S. (1996). *The Cultural Contradictions of Motherhood*. United States: Yale University Press.

Malacrida, C. (2009). *Performing Motherhood in a Disablist World: Dilemmas of Motherhood, Femininity and Disability.* International Journal of Qualitative Studies in Education: Vol. 22, pp. 99–117.

Oakley, A. (1984). *Taking It Like a Woman.* United States: Random House.

O.Reilly, A. (2004). *From Motherhood to Mothering: The Legacy of Adrienne Rich's Of Woman Born*. New York, United States: SUNY Press.

Orenstein, P. (2000). *Flux: Women on Sex, Work, Love, Kids and Life in a Half-Changed World*. New York, United States. Anchor Books.

Reich, J. A. (2014). *Neoliberal Mothering and Vaccine Refusal: Imagined Gated Communities and the Privilege of Choice*. Gender & Society: Vol. 22, pp. 202–226.

Senior, J. (2014). *All Joy and No Fun: The Paradox of Modern Parenthood*. United States: HarperCollins Publishing.

Suissa, J. & Ramaekers, S. (2012). *The Claims of Parenting*. Netherlands: Springer.

Takševa, T. (2018). *Motherhood Studies and Feminist Theory: Elisions and Intersections*. Journal of the Motherhood Initiative: Vol. 9(1).

Taylor, T. (2011). *Re-examining Cultural Contradictions: Mothering, Ideology, and the Intersections of Class, Gender, and*

Race. Sociology Compass: Vol. 10(5), pp. 898–907.

Taussig, R. (2020). *Sitting Pretty: The View from My Ordinary Resilient Disabled Body*. United States: HarperCollins Publishing.

Tichenor, V., McQuillan, J., Griel, A. L., Bedrous, A. V., Clark, A., & Shreffler, K. M. (2016). *Variation in Attitudes toward Being a Mother by Race/Ethnicity and Education among Women in the United States*. Sociological Perspectives.

THE NOISE SAYS MOTHERS MUST BE SELFLESS

Athan, A. (2016). 'How Academia Studies Mothers'. *Every Mother Counts*. [Online article].

Brown, E. (2016). 'Music and Change'. *Change Making Women*. [Online article].

Collins English Dictionary. (2018). Glasgow: HarperCollins Publishers.

Conley, M. (2020). 'Motherhood in America Is a Multi Level Marketing Scheme. *GEN Medium*. [Online article].

Dionne, E. (2015). 'For Black Women, Self-Care Is A Radical Act'. *Ravishly*. [Online article].

Lorde, A. (2017). *A Burst of Light: And Other Essays*. United States: DOVER.

Mintz, S. (2017). 'How Childhood Has Changed (and How That Impacts Education)'. *EdSurge*. [Online article].

Oliver, M. (1995). *Blue Pastures*. United Kingdom: Cengage Learning EMEA.

O'Reilly, A. (2014). *Mothers, Mothering and Motherhood Across Cultural Differences*. Canada: Demeter Press.

Rhimes, S. (2015). *Year of Yes: How to Dance It Out, Stand In the Sun and Be Your Own Person*. United Kingdom: Simon & Schuster.

THE NOISE SAYS MOTHERS MUST MAKE OUR CHILDREN HAPPY

Dodd, C. (1997). 'Planning for a Superbaby'. *The Independent*. [Online article].

Douglas, D. & Michaels, M.(2005). *The Mommy Myth: The Idealization of*

Motherhood and How It Has Undermined Women. United States: FREE PR.

Senior, J. (2014). *All Joy and No Fun: The Paradox of Modern Parenthood.* United States: HarperCollins Publishing.

Urbaniak, K. (2020). 'The Making of the Good Girl'. *KasiaUrbaniak.com.* [Online Article].

Weale, S. (2020). 'Youth Services Suffer 70% Funding Cut in Less than a Decade'. *The Guardian.* [Online article].

THE NOISE SAYS MOTHERS WILL FEEL GUILTY

Crowley, J. E. (2014). *Staying at Home or Working for Pay? Attachment to Modern Mothering Identities.* Sociological Spectrum: Vol. 34(2), pp.114–135.

Douglas, D. & Michaels, M. (2005). *The Mommy Myth: The Idealisation of Motherhood and How It Has Undermined Women.* United States: FREE PR.

Drentea, P. & Moren Cross, J. (2011). 'Online Motherhood: A Community of Mothers

Revisited' in Moravec, M. (Ed). *Motherhood Online*. United Kingdom: Cambridge Scholars Publishing.

Duncan, S., Edwards, R., Reynolds, T., & Alldred, P. (2004). *Mothers and Child Care: Policies, Values and Theories*. Children and Society: Vol.18(4), pp. 245–265.

Edison Research & Triton Digital. (2020). An Infinite Dial Report on Moms and Media.

Faris, A. (March, 2015). 'The Mom Star in the Day that Changed Her Life'. *Redbook Magazine*. [Print Article].

Greer, G. (2013). Guilt Poisons Women. *Edition CNN*. [Online article].

Jong, E. (1973). *Fear of Flying*. Edinburgh, United Kingdom: Canongate Books Ltd

Liss, M., Schiffrin, H. H., & Rizzo, K. M. (2012). *Maternal Guilt and Shame: The Role of Self-discrepancy and Fear of Negative Evaluation*. Journal of Child and Family Studies.

Lorde, A. (1981). *Sister Outsider: Essays and Speeches*. Berkeley, United States: Random House.

O'Connor, L. E., Berry, J. W., Weiss, J. & Gilbert, P. (2002). *Guilt, Fear, Submission, and Empathy in Depression*. Journal of Affective Disorders: Vol. 71, Issues 1–3.

O'Reilly, A. (2004). *Mother Outlaws: Theories and Practices of Empowered Mothering*. United Kingdom: Women's Press UK.

Rich, A. (1976). *Of Woman Born: Motherhood as Experience and Institution*. New York, United States: WW Norton & Co.

Seagram, S. & Daniluk, J. C. (2002). *"It goes with the territory": The Meaning and Experience of Maternal Guilt for Mothers of Preadolescent Children*. Women & Therapy: Vol. 25, pp. 61–88.

Swigart, J. (1998). *The Myth of the Bad Mother: Parenting Without Guilt*. United States: Contemporary Book Publishing.

THE NOISE SAYS MOTHERS AMBITION SHRINKS

Abouzahr, K., Krentz, M., Taplett, F., Tracey, C. & Tsusaka, M. (2017). Dispelling the

Myths of the Gender "Ambition Gap"'. *Boston Consulting Group Study*.

Arnold, F. (2019). 'Female Ambition: Psychoanalytic Perspectives' in Arnold, F. & Brody, S. (Eds). *Psychoanalytic Perspectives on Women and Their Experience of Desire, Ambition and Leadership*. United Kingdom: Taylor & Francis Ltd.

Brody, S. (2019). *Psychoanalytic Perspectives on Women and Their Experience of Desire, Ambition and Leadership*. United Kingdom: Taylor & Francis Ltd.

Budig, M. J. & Hodges, M. J. (2010). *Differences in Disadvantage: Variation in the Motherhood Penalty across White Women's Earnings Distribution*. American Sociological Review: Vol. 75(5), pp. 705–728.

Cambridge Dictionary. (2020). United Kingdom: Cambridge University Press.

Dinnerstein, D. (1999). *The Mermaid and the Minotaur*. New York, United States: Other Press.

Equality and Human Rights Commission.

(2016). 'Pregnancy and Maternity –
Related Discrimination and Disadvantage:
Experiences of Mothers'.

Faulkner, S. (2012). *That Baby Will Cost
You: An Intended Ambivalent Pregnancy*.
Qualitative Inquiry: Vol. 18(4).

Glynn, S. J. (2017). 'Breadwinning Mothers
Are Increasingly the U.S. Norm'.
Washington Center for American Progress.

Haffert, K. (2019). 'The Enthusiasm Gap
Between Men and Women'. *Green
Connections Radio*.

Harris, A. (1997). *Aggression, Envy, and
Ambition: Circulating Tensions in Women's
Psychic Life*. Gender & Psychoanalysis: Vol.
2, pp. 291–325.

Hewlett, S. A. & Marshall, M. (2015). *Women
Want Five Things*. United States: Center For
Talent Innovation.

Holmes, D. (2019). 'A Case of the Othering
of a Woman's Ambition' in Arnold, F. &
Brody, S. (Eds). *Psychoanalytic Perspectives
on Women and Their Experience of Desire,*

Ambition and Leadership. United Kingdom: Taylor & Francis Ltd.

Holmes, E. K., Erickson, J. J., Hill, E. J. (2012). *Doing What She Thinks is Best: Maternal Psychological Wellbeing and Attaining Desired Work Situations*. Human Relations: Vol. 65(4), pp. 501–522.

Layton, L. (2004). *Dreams of America/ American Dreams*. Psychoanalytic Dialogues: Vol. 14, pp. 233–254.

Lewis, P. (2014). *Postfeminism, Femininities and Organization Studies: Exploring a New Agenda*. Organization Studies: Vol. 35(12), pp. 1845–1866.

Lorde, A. (1985). *Poetry is Not a Luxury.* United States: Druck & Verlags Cooperative.

Marshall, M. & Wingfield, T. (2016). *Ambition in Black + White: The Feminist Narrative (Revised).* Los Angeles, United States: Rare Bird Books.

National Women's Law Center. (2017). 'A Snapshot of Working Mothers'.

Nikunen, M. (2014). *The 'Entrepreneurial*

University', Family and Gender: Changes and Demands Faced by Fixed-Term Workers. Gender and Education: Vol. 26(2).

van Amsterdam, N. (2015). *Othering the 'Leaky Body': An Autoethnographic Story About Expressing Breast Milk in the Workplace.* Culture and Organization: Vol. 21(3).

Powell, D. (2019). 'Appropriated Ambition….a Narrative' in Arnold, F. & Brody, S. (Eds). *Psychoanalytic Perspectives on Women and Their Experience of Desire, Ambition and Leadership.* United Kingdom: Taylor & Francis Ltd.

Rodsky, E. (2019). *Fair Play: Share the Mental Load, Rebalance Your Relationship and Transform Your Life.* United Kingdom: Quercus Publishing Plc.

Sandberg, S. (2013) *Lean In: Women, Work, and the Will to Lead.* United Kingdom: Random House.

Slater and Gordon Law Firm Survey. (2014). '40% of Managers Avoid Hiring Younger Women to Get Around Maternity Leave'. *The Guardian.* [Online article].

Seals Allers, K. (2018). 'Rethinking Work-Life Balance for Women of Color'. *SLATE*. [Online article].

Sutherland, J. A. (2006). *What Can I Do Different, What Could Be Better, What Could You Do More?*. Guilt, Shame and Mothering.

Turner, P. & Norwood, K. (2014). '"*I had the luxury …*": *Organizational Breastfeeding Support as Privatized Privilege*. Human Relations: Vol. 67(7).

THE NOISE SAYS MOTHERS MUST BE SEXLESS & SEXY

Bologna, C. (2016). Meet The Breastfeeding Pole Dancer Who Takes Multitasking To New Heights. *Huffington Post*. [Online article].

Cass, V. (2020). The Myth of Asexual Motherhood. In H. Zwalf, M.Walks & J. Mortenson (Eds) *Mothers, sex and sexuality*. United States: Demeter Press

Friedman, M. (2014). Unpacking MILF: Exploring motherhood, sexuality &

feminism. *Atlantis: A Women's Studies Journal*, 36.2 pp. 49–60.

Halberstam, J. J. (2011). *The Queer Art of Failure*. United States: Duke University Press Books.

Johnson, J. K. (2021). Sexual Mother. *Magamama.com*. [Online article].

Ketz, K. (2001). An Examination of Sexual Self concept and Body Image in Predominantly Caucasian Lesbian and Heterosexual Women with Physical Disabilities. Division 44, American Psychological Association, *Society for the Study of Lesbian, Gay and Bisexual Issues*. Vol 17,3, pp. 3–5.

Longhurst, R. (2011). *Maternities: Gender, Bodies and Space*. UK: Routledge.

Lorde, A. (2013). *Sister Outsider: Essays and Speeches*. United States: Ten Speed Press Reprint.

Loubriel, J. (2015). 6 Things You're Actually Saying When You Reduce Latinas to the 'Spicy' Stereotype. *EverydayFeminism.com*. [Online article].

Malina, D., & Schmidt, R. (1997). It's Business Doing Pleasure With You: Sh! A women's sex shop case. *Marketing Intelligence & Planning.* Vol. 15: 7, pp. 352–360.

Martin, N. K. (2007). Porn Empowerment: Negotiating Sex Work and Third Wave Feminism. *Atlantis: A Women's Studies Journal.* Vol. 31: 2, pp. 31–41.

Moran, C. (2011). *How to be a Woman,* London: Ebury Press.

Parliament UK (25 June 2020). *Improve Maternal Mortality Rates and Health Care for Black Women in the U.K.* [Online article].

Perel, E. (2007). *Mating in Captivity: Sex, Lies and Domestic Bliss.* Great Britain: HarperCollins Publishers.

Pinterics, N. (2020). Excessive Maternal Embodiment: The Queer Danger of Desirous Mothers. In H. Zwalf, M.Walks & J. Mortenson (Eds). *Mothers, Sex & Sexuality.* United States: Demeter Press.

Rich, A. (1996). *Of Woman Born: Motherhood*

as Experience and Institution. London: W.W. Norton & Company Ltd.

Roberts, D. (2002). *Shattered bonds: The color of child welfare.* New York, NY: Basic Civitas Books.

Rogers, J. (2005). *The Disabled Woman's Guide to Pregnancy and Birth.* New York, NY: Demos Medical Publishing.

Rosenthal, L. & Lobel, M. (2011). Explaining racial disparities in adverse birth outcomes: unique sources of stress for Black American women. *Social Science & Medicine.* Vol. 72, pp. 977–983.

Shavers, V. L., Fagan, P., Jones, D., Klein, W. M., Boyington, J., Moten, C., & Rorie, E. (2012). The state of research on racial/ethnic discrimination in the receipt of health care. *American Journal of Public Health.* Vol. 102, pp. 953–966.

Sublette, N., & Sublette, C. (2015). *The American slave coast: A history of the slave-breeding industry.* Chicago, IL: Lawrence Hill Books

Sundahl, D. (2003). *Female Ejaculation: THE*

G-SPOT. United States: Hunter House, Inc.

Taussig, R. (2020) *Sitting Pretty: The View from My Ordinary Resilient Disabled Body*. San Francisco: HarperOne.

Thompson, J. (2002). *Mommy Queerest: Contemporary Rhetorics of Lesbian Maternal Identity.* United States: University Massachusetts Press.

Waheed, N. (2014). *nejma.* Scotts Valley: CreateSpace Independent Publishing Platform.

Wolny, N. (2019). The LGBTQ+ Community Has $3.7 Trillion In Purchasing Power; Here's How We Want You to Sell to Us. *Entrepreneur.* [Online article].

Young, I. M. (2005). *On Female Body Experience: "Throwing Like A Girl" and other Essays.* New York: Oxford University Press.

Zwalf, H. (2020). Mothers, Sex & Sexuality: A Sexy Book. In H. Zwalf, M.Walks & J. Mortenson (Eds). *Mothers, Sex & Sexuality.* United States: Demeter Press

THE FUTURE: NOISE & MOTHERHOOD

Blundell, R., Costa Dias, M., Joyce, R., Xu, X. (2020). *Covid-19 and Inequalities*. Fiscal Studies: Vol. 41(2).

Dias, F. A., Chance, J. & Buchanan, A. (2020). *The Motherhood Penalty and The Fatherhood Premium in Employment during Covid-19: Evidence from The United States*. Science Direct.

Doyle, G. (2020). *Untamed: Stop Pleasing, Start Living*. New York, United States: The Dial Press.

Hardwicke Collings, J. (2018). 'On Turning 60'. *Jane Hardwicke Collings*. [Online article].

Independent, (2018). 'As We Continue to Blame Single Mothers for Society's Woes, it's No Surprise Their Children are Living in Poverty'. *Independent Voices*. [Online Article].

Lean In & McKinsey & Co. (2020). Women in the Workplace: Corporate America is at a Critical Crossroads'. *Empower Women*. [Online article].

Malkia A Cyril, M. A. (2016). 'Motherhood, Media, and Building a 21st-Century Movement' in Gumbs, A. P., Martens, C., & Williams, M. (Eds). *Revolutionary Mothering: Love on the Front Lines*. United States: PM Press.

Myers, K. (2020). *Raising Them: Our Adventure in Gender Creative Parenting*. United States: Amazon Publishing.

Peters, J. (1997). *When Mothers Work: Loving Our Children Without Sacrificing Our Selves*. United Kingdom: Da Capo Lifelong Books.

Platt, L. & Warwick, R. (2020). *COVID-19 and Ethnic Inequalities in England and Wales*. Fiscal Studies: Vol. 4(2).

Rodsky, E. (2019). *Fair Play: Share the Mental Load, Rebalance Your Relationship and Transform Your Life*. United Kingdom: Quercus Publishing Plc.

Sandberg, S. (2021). 'We Need to Use the Pandemic to Finally Get Gender Equality Right'. *Wired*. [Online article].

School for Mothers Special Report. (2020). 'Mothers & COVID-19'. *School for Mothers.*

SPUNK: A Manifesto Modernising Fatherhood

Danusia Malina-Derben
NOVEMBER 2021
www.triumphpress.co/spunk